LAW
ENFORCEMENT
AGENCIES

THE SECRET SERVICE

LAW ENFORCEMENT AGENCIES

Bomb Squad

Border Patrol

Federal Bureau of Investigation

The Secret Service

SWAT Teams

The Texas Rangers

LAW
ENFORCEMENT
A G E N C I E S

THE SECRET
SERVICE

Bernard Ryan Jr.

CHELSEA HOUSE
P U B L I S H E R S
An imprint of Infobase Publishing

THE SECRET SERVICE

Chelsea House
An imprint of Infobase Publishing
132 West 31st Street
New York NY 10001

Library of Congress Cataloging-in-Publication Data

Ryan, Bernard, 1923–
The Secret Service / Bernard Ryan, Jr.
p. cm. — (Law enforcement agencies)
Includes bibliographical references and index.
ISBN-13: 978-1-60413-623-4 (hardcover : alk. paper)
ISBN-10: 1-60413-623-5 (hardcover : alk. paper) 1. United States. Secret Service—
Juvenile literature. 2. Secret service—United States—Juvenile literature. I. Title. II. Series.
HV8144.S43R93 2010   363.28'30973—dc22
2010029372

Chelsea House books are available at special discounts when purchased
in bulk quantities for businesses, associations, institutions,
or sales promotions. Please call our Special Sales Department
in New York at (212) 967-8800 or (800) 322-8755.

You can find Chelsea House on the World Wide Web at http://www.chelseahouse.com

Text design and composition by Erika K. Arroyo
Cover deign by Keith Trego
Cover printed by Bang Printing, Brainerd, Minn.
Book printed and bound by Bang Printing, Brainerd, Minn.
Date printed: December 2010

Printed in the United States of America

10 9 8 7 6 5 4 3 2 1

This book is printed on acid-free paper.

All links and Web addresses were checked and verified to be correct
at the time of publication. Because of the dynamic nature of the Web,
some addresses and links may have changed since publication and may no longer be valid.

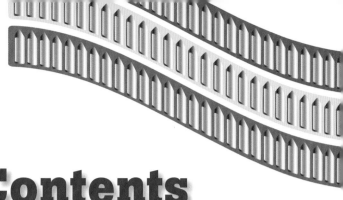

Contents

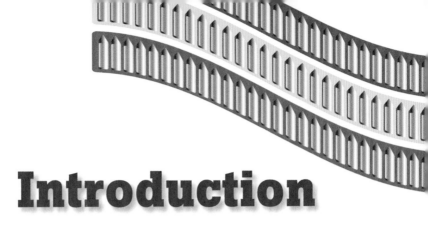

Introduction

Of all the key police agencies, teams, and organizations, perhaps the most challenging to be a part of is the United States Secret Service. Why? Because a Secret Service man or woman may reach the position where he or she is directly responsible for protecting the life of the president of the United States or of the vice president as well as their families. Being a Secret Service agent is a job requiring a wide range of skills, an extremely strong sense of devotion to duty, a top-notch level of intelligence, and the utmost bravery in the face of immediate danger.

Protecting the key people in the United States government is not, however, the sole purpose of the Secret Service. Its agents work in a variety of other jobs not only in the nation's capital but also across the country. This book is organized into chapters that describe the diversity of Secret Service work, including many specific examples of events that have occurred in the experience of Secret Service agents and other staff members.

Chapter 1, "The Big Picture," presents an overview of the Secret Service and its role as an arm of the United States Department of Homeland Security.

Chapter 2, "How the Secret Service Began," recounts the history of the Secret Service from its founding in 1865 as a solution to the problem of counterfeiting. The chapter reveals why the service was established under the Department of the Treasury and shows how it grew because of smugglers and moonshiners. The expansion of protection to others beyond the occupants of the White House, and the widening of the investigative work to include such sophisticated crimes as identity theft and telemarketing fraud, complete the chapter.

The agency's primary work of protecting people, buildings, and areas is described in Chapter 3, "Protecting People and Places."

Chapter 4, "Investigating Counterfeiting and Fraud," takes the reader into the investigative work of the Secret Service. It shows how the agency identifies and charges individuals involved in a wide range of nonviolent crimes, from counterfeiting of United States currency to identity theft.

Chapter 5, "Recognizing a Threat," looks into the Secret Service's National Threat Assessment Center, detailing its skills in identifying, assessing, and managing people who may be determined to attack public officials or even everyday teachers and pupils in schools.

Chapter 6, "Handling Crowds and Major Events," concentrates on a special area of Secret Service activity that dates from the administration of President Bill Clinton: major events that evoke nationwide interest.

Chapter 7, "What It Takes to Learn How," details how Secret Service agents learn their job. Included are inside looks at the basic training courses held at both the Federal Law Enforcement Training Center in New Mexico and the agency's own James J. Rowley Training Center in Maryland.

Chapter 8, "On the Job," takes the reader on the job with a number of Secret Service agents. It shows what kind of person "the consummate agent" is, why agents may get assignments that are unpleasant, and how agents have coped with stressful incidents.

This book's final chapter, "The Future of the Secret Service," looks briefly at the standing of the Secret Service in the second decade of the 20th century.

The Big Picture

Everyone knows that the men and women of the Secret Service guard the president of the United States from harm. What most people don't know is that Secret Service agents perform a wide variety of other duties to prevent and help solve crimes. The duties can be summed up under two basic spheres of responsibility: protection and investigation. One might think of it a little more broadly in this way: Preventing crimes involves protecting people and places so crimes don't happen, but when crimes do happen, or are suspected of occurring, investigation involves figuring out what did happen or what may be occurring.

A MAJOR PART OF HOMELAND SECURITY

The people who do this work are employed by the U.S. government in its Department of Homeland Security. One of several agencies in the department, in 2010 the Secret Service had approximately 3,200 special agents, 1,300 members of its Uniformed Division, and more than 2,000 technical, professional, and administrative support staff. Its annual budget is $1.487 billion.[1] Depending on their current assignments, some Secret Service agents wear uniforms while at work. Others are in civilian clothes. The assignments are not permanent. An agent may work for a period of time in one protective assignment wearing a uniform, then for another time in a protective assignment in civilian clothes. Agents doing investigative work are usually dressed as civilians. During his or her career, every agent must be willing to carry out assignments in both

A uniformed Secret Service agent stands guard in front of the north portico of the White House. *(Brooks Kraft/Corbis)*

protective and investigative work. The unique dual aspects of the job—the protective side and the investigative side—make the Secret Service distinctive from other law enforcement agencies.

Some may think that working for the Secret Service means living and working in Washington, D.C., but the agency has offices in the nation's capital and across the continental United States and in Alaska, Hawaii, and Puerto Rico. Affiliated or liaison (closely connected) offices are in London, England; Paris, France; Bonn, Germany; Rome and Milan, Italy; Hong Kong, China; Ottawa, Montreal, and Vancouver, Canada; Nicosia, Cyprus; Bogota, Colombia; Manila, Philippines; and Bangkok, Thailand.

In the course of a career, any Secret Service agent must be available for assignment to any of these worldwide duty stations. With training and experience in all aspects of the work, any agent is expected to know what to do when needed in any protective or investigative assignment anywhere.

WHO MIGHT BE A THREAT?

For many years, the Secret Service has believed that the best way to protect a person or place from harm is to prevent an attack from

GENERAL ORDERS DATING FROM 1865

When the Secret Service's first Chief (as he was then known), William P. Wood, took office in July 1865, he outlined the moral and legal obligations of every agent (note that it did not occur to Chief Wood that some agents might someday be women):

1. Each man must recognize that his service belongs to the government 24 hours a day.
2. All must agree to assignment to locations chosen by the chief and respond to whatever mobility of movement the work might require.
3. All must exercise such careful saving of money spent for travel, subsistence, and payments for information as can be self-evidently justified.
4. Continuing employment in the Secret Service will depend upon demonstrated fitness, ability as investigators, and honesty and fidelity in all transactions.
5. The title of regular employees will be operative, Secret Service. Temporary employees will be assistant operatives or informants.
6. All employment will be as a daily pay rate; accounts submitted monthly. Each operative will be expected to keep on hand enough personal reserve funds to carry on Service business between paydays.

occurring in the first place. Therefore it works hard to identify persons who have an interest in mounting attacks against those whom the service protects. In the process, it analyzes the ability of such persons to mount attacks, and tries to manage them. Its National Threat Assessment Center (NTAC) handles this work, maintaining continuing research into attacks that have been made on public officials, on other public figures, and in schools. To help other law enforcement officials who are responsible for public safety and for protecting individuals, NTAC trains them on how to assess threats and possible violence in such areas as schools and workplaces, which are typical targets of would-be attackers.

NTAC maintains several ongoing projects and studies. Its Exceptional Case Study Project (ECSP) looks at the thinking and behavior of people who have assassinated, attacked, or tried to attack public figures. School shootings and other attacks based in schools are analyzed by its Safe School Initiative (SSI). Following up on the SSI, NTAC's Bystander Study has concentrated on students and others who knew when school violence was planned but didn't say anything. Another project, the Insider Threat Study (ITS), has looked at those who are inside organizations—those, for example, who are current or former employees—and have purposely harmed them. Still another program is designed to help all law enforcement agencies in matters involving children who are missing or who are being exploited. Called Operation Safe Kids, it uses up-to-date technology to record vital information that identifies children who may be taken advantage of or may become missing.

SPECIAL EVENTS OF NATIONAL SIGNIFICANCE

Suppose the Pope is planning a trip to America from Italy, with a long, busy schedule of public appearances. Or suppose that next January 20 a major once-every-four-years event—the inauguration of a president of the United States—will occur. By a federal law, the Secret Service is in charge of planning, coordinating, and implementing the security operations for such events and many others. Who decides whether an event is important enough to get such attention? The Secretary of Homeland Security designates it as a National Special Security Event (NSSE) and

Secret Service agents walk alongside the presidential limousine transporting President Barack Obama and First Lady Michelle Obama down the parade route on Pennsylvania Avenue on inauguration day. *(AP Photo/Charles Dharapak)*

the Secret Service goes to work lining up partnerships with law enforcement agencies and public safety officials at all levels—federal, state, and local. Getting ready for such events takes tremendous planning and coordination, especially with regard to training all those who will be on duty, lining up communications facilities, checking for authorized credentials, and making sure that the motorcade routes to gathering places, and the places themselves, can be made secure.

How the Secret Service Began

It is early in the 20th century. Quentin Roosevelt, 12 years old and the youngest son of President Theodore Roosevelt, and several of his schoolmates are riding their bikes along Massachusetts Avenue in Washington. Quentin notices a man who seems determined to watch him and his friends. He tells his pals to distract the stranger, then with his bicycle runs into him and demands, "Why have you been hanging around?"

"I'm sorry, Quentin," says the man. "But I'm under orders."

"You think you can boss my father and my mother," says Quentin, "but you can't boss me. I don't need any of your attention, not with this bunch trailing along."

Years later, one of the bunch writes, "We knew little of the watchful care with which our movements—especially about the White House grounds—were followed. We knew there were electrical push-buttons in various strategic places, and signal devices, by which the guard was informed where to concentrate; but the most assiduous searching and persistent questioning failed to reveal to us one single piece of evidence of the character of the mechanism by which this invisible guardianship was controlled. It was, and is, a remarkably efficient, well considered system."[1]

Probably the best-known duty of the United States Secret Service is the task of protecting the president and his family. This, however, is not the work for which the Secret Service was first set up. By coincidence, the service was founded on July 5, 1865, only a few weeks after President Abraham Lincoln was assassinated on April 14th by actor John Wilkes Booth. If the Secret Service as we know it today had been on duty at Ford's Theater in Washington on that evening, Booth would not have been able to sneak up behind the president as he and Mrs. Lincoln watched the performance of the play *Our American Cousin.*

3,000 KINDS OF MONEY

The Secret Service was formed to solve a problem that was totally different from protecting the president. For fourscore and six years, from 1776 until 1862, the United States had not had any standard money printed by the government. All paper money in use during those years was printed privately by individual banks. With some 3,000 banks each using their own designs, there was great temptation for counterfeiters—people who design and print fake money. By the end of the Civil War in April 1865, between one-third and one-half of all paper money in circulation in the United States was counterfeit.

In 1862 Congress passed an act that allowed the United States to print money and control its supply. In the meantime, it had passed several laws, over many years, to suppress counterfeiting. But our lawmakers had not approved any funds to enforce the laws.

Now it was up to Congress to protect the new money against counterfeiters. On July 5, 1865, it established the U.S. Secret Service as a bureau under the Department of the Treasury. People known as Secret Service agents went to work. They investigated the sources of counterfeit money all across America, arresting designers and printers who broke the law and bringing them to trial. In fewer than 10 years, counterfeiting was sharply reduced and American citizens felt much more secure about the money they used to buy and sell goods.

SMUGGLERS AND MOONSHINERS

The Department of the Treasury was responsible for collecting taxes to keep the government running. As a result, it needed to investigate

(Continues on page 18)

1996 style consists of series years 1996, 1999, 2001, 2003, 2003A and 2006.

2004 style incorporates background color and consists of series years 2004, 2004A and 2006.

Paper Currency paper consists of 25% linen and 75% cotton and contains small randomly disbursed red and blue fibers embedded throughout the paper.

Portrait The 1996 style Federal Reserve Notes (FRNs) have an enlarged and off-center portrait enclosed in an oval frame of concentric lines. The 2004 style FRNs have an enlarged and off-center portrait without a frame.

① **Watermark** The 1996 and 2004 style FRNs have a watermark that is visible from either side when held up to a light source.

② **Color-Shifting Ink** The 1996 style FRNs have color-shifting ink in the lower right-hand corner, that shifts from green to black as the note is tilted 45 degrees. The 2004 style $10, $20 and $50 FRNs have color-shifting ink that shifts from copper to green as the note is tilted 45 degrees. The $5 FRN does not have color-shifting ink.

③ **Security Thread** Genuine FRNs have a clear polyester thread embedded vertically in the paper. The thread is inscribed with the denomination of the note, and is visible only when held up to light. Each denomination has a unique thread position and will glow a unique color in ultraviolet (UV) light.

④ **Serial Numbers** The first letter of the serial number on FRNs corresponds to the series year.

Under a UV light source, the security thread glows light red/pink.

1996 Style		**2004 Style**
A=1996	D= 2003	E= 2004
B=1999	F= 2003A	G = 2004A
C=2001	H= 2006	I= 2006

Under a UV light source, the security thread glows yellow.

Bank Indicators

⑤ **Federal Reserve Indicators** The 1996 style and 2004 style FRNs have a letter-number combination, which identifies one of the 12 issuing Federal Reserve Banks. This letter-number combination appears beneath the serial number on the left. The number corresponds to the position of the letter in the alphabet, e.g.: A1, B2, C3, etc. The second letter of the serial number is the same as the letter in the letter-number combination.

⑥ **Check Letter/ Quadrant Number**

⑦ **Face Plate Number**

⑧ **Series Year**

⑨ **Back Plate Number** *(Not shown)* Found on the reverse right hand side of the note.

April 2008

Under a UV light source, the security thread glows green.

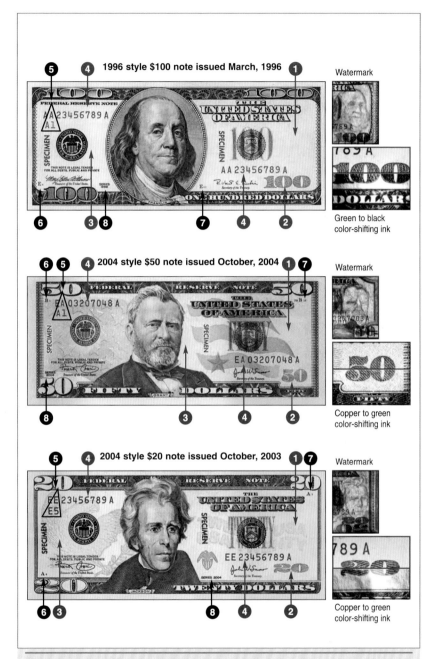

(Facing pages) The Secret Service released the "Know Your Money" public information brochure in April 2008 to help the public recognize counterfeit currency. *(United States Secret Service)*

(Continued from page 15)

many activities in which people managed to avoid paying taxes they owed or made a product without getting a required license to do so. One example of such activities was the unlicensed brewing or distilling of such alcoholic beverages as beer or whiskey, which were taxable. Their makers became known as "moonshiners" and their illegal drink was called "moonshine," because the distillers operated at night by the light of the moon. Those words are still in use today.

Another example was the smuggling of alcoholic drinks and other products into the United States without paying customs taxes on them. Secret Service agents soon became known for their success in investigating such operations and stopping them.

At the time when the Secret Service was founded, the federal government had no office or agency in charge of enforcing federal laws. Within two years, by 1867, many government departments other than the Treasury were requesting the use of Secret Service agents to investigate violations of their laws. So Secret Service duties were expanded to include "detecting persons perpetrating frauds against the government." What is fraud? It is purposely lying in order to get someone to part with something of value or to give up a legal right. A fraudulent act or activity is based on, or done by, using fraud. If a person is a fraud, that person is not what he or she pretends to be.

This change broadened the agents' field of service. Now, with more and more railroads being built across America, agents were put in charge of investigating mail robberies. And, as the U.S. government—under a law called the Homestead Act of 1862—gave free land to people willing to be pioneers moving westward, the Secret Service investigated land frauds.

SPYING ON THE SPIES

Secret Service duties were extended even more in 1898, during the Spanish-American War. American leaders learned that a ring of spies for Spain was operating against the United States from somewhere in Canada. The U.S. Secret Service organized a counterespionage group. Its investigators found the spy headquarters in Montreal. They exposed Lieutenant Ramon Carranza, a representative of the Spanish navy who was on duty in the Spanish embassy in Canada, as the spy ring's mastermind. Carranza was banished from Canada by its government, and other spies in the United States were arrested. That ended the Spanish spy system.

For some 35 years after it was founded, the Secret Service continued to chase down counterfeiters, bootleggers, makers of moonshine whiskey, and people who could be accused of fraud against the U.S. government. But the assassination of President William McKinley in 1901 brought a major change in the agency's duties. It was ordered by Congress to protect McKinley's successor, President Theodore Roosevelt.

Secret Service men walk on each side of the carriage for President Theodore Roosevelt's inauguration parade on March 4, 1905. After the assassination of President William McKinley in 1901, Congress added the protection of the president to the Secret Service's duties. *(Bettmann/Corbis)*

While Congress quickly gave the Secret Service the job of protecting the president, it did not provide funds to pay for the work until, in 1906, it passed the Sundry Civil Expenses Act for 1907. And not until 1913 did it authorize permanent protection of the president and of the president-elect as official duties of the Secret Service. Protection of the president's immediate family was not authorized by Congress until 1917.

TOO MANY ASSASSINATIONS

In 1901 the city of Buffalo, New York, held an international fair called the Pan-American Exposition (because it was host to most of the countries of North and South America). The giant exhibition included displays of the products made and the arts and crafts created in the various nations.

At the exposition on September 5, U.S. President William McKinley made an important speech, detailing the problems that he saw facing our nation and proposing his ideas for solving them. On the next day, at a reception in the Music Hall of the exposition, he was shot twice by anarchist Leon Czolgosz. McKinley died eight days later, and Vice President Theodore Roosevelt took his place as president.

Only 20 years before that, on July 2, 1881, President James Abram Garfield had been shot while in the waiting room of the Baltimore and Potomac Railroad station in Washington on the way to deliver the commencement speech at his alma mater, Williams College, in Massachusetts. He lived, suffering painfully, until September 19th. His assassin, Charles Jules Guiteau, was a Chicago lawyer who had gone to Washington expecting to be named U.S. consul (an official who represents the interests of our citizens in another country) at Marseilles, France. Disappointed at not getting the job, Guiteau took his anger out on the president. He was tried and convicted of murder and was hanged on June 30, 1882.

Only 16 years earlier, on April 14, 1865, actor John Wilkes Booth had easily and boldly stepped into the booth in Ford's

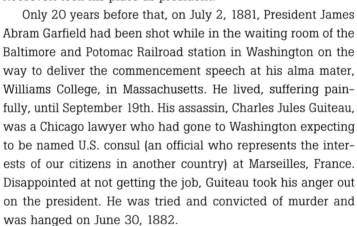

LOUISIANA LOTTERY: FROM LEGAL TO ILLEGAL

In the years from 1902 to 1908, Secret Service agents were borrowed by the Department of Justice, which needed help in suppressing illegal lotteries. The problem had begun with a lottery that was legal. Known as the Louisiana Lottery, it had been organized in New Orleans during the

Theatre in Washington and shot President Abraham Lincoln as he watched the play *Our American Cousin*.

With the deaths of Lincoln, Garfield, and McKinley, the United States had seen three assassinations of its presidents in 36 years. Reacting to the public's outrage, Congress turned to an established federal law enforcement organization: the U.S. Secret Service. In 1901 it passed a resolution requesting Secret Service protection for the new president, Theodore Roosevelt.

A crowd gathers on the street to watch the coffin of President William McKinley being transferred to a hearse after his funeral services in September 1901. *(Corbis)*

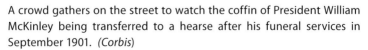

Civil War with the approval of the Louisiana government, which permitted it to authorize a number of people as lottery owners. During the three decades following the war, the lottery owners had taken in about $300 million but had paid out only a small amount to lottery winners. By controlling the winning numbers, and through various other dishonest practices, so many lottery owners had become multimillionaires that the State of Louisiana ended the Louisiana Lottery in 1892.

That did not stop the lottery owners. They moved their headquarters to the city of Puerto Cortez, in Honduras, but kept offices in several cities in the United States. They used a printing plant in Tampa, Florida, to print lottery tickets, and owned a steamship, *The Breakwater*, that regularly carried lottery results between Tampa, New Orleans, and Puerto Cortez.

To combat this operation, Congress passed a new law. In 1895 it prohibited the sending of lottery materials or information by mail. The lottery owners met that challenge by paying trusted messengers to distribute lottery tickets across the United States.

Determined to suppress this illegal activity, the Justice Department brought in Secret Service agents in 1902. Over six years, the agents seized many thousands of illegal lottery tickets and made hundreds of arrests. By 1908, they had eradicated what was left of the Louisiana Lottery.

While Department of Justice officials appreciated the work the Secret Service agents did in tracking down and arresting the operators of illegal lotteries, by 1905 it identified yet another problem. To help solve it, Attorney General William H. Moody asked the Secret Service to lend 32 agents to the Justice Department.

HOMESTEADERS WHO DID NOT MAKE HOMES

The problem was that people were abusing the privileges that were provided by the Homestead Act of 1862. The purpose of the act was to encourage people to move west and settle the vast public lands of the United States as it grew. Under the law, any United States citizen could apply to get 160 acres of land free of charge. The settler was required to make that land his home, and not live anywhere else, for three years. At the end of that time, he had to give proof that he had lived there and had cultivated and improved the land. Then the U.S. government would give him full title—that is, ownership—of the land; until then, it was still the government's land.

Over the years, however, many frauds were committed. Wealthy owners of cattle set up phony settlers to claim rich grazing lands and then used the lands for their herds to roam across. Other dishonest landowners pretended they were farming the land but actually were mining coal, pumping oil, and felling trees to sell for lumber.

The 32 Secret Service agents began investigating fraud committed under the Homestead Act. It was tough and even dangerous work. For example, in Durango, Colorado, Agent Joseph A. Walker suspected that coal was being mined and sold from a homesteader's claim, which was government property. He and another agent, along with a representative from the U.S. Department of the Interior and a coal miner, were inspecting the claim on November 3, 1907, when they discovered a large hole in the ground. While the other three descended by rope into the hole, Walker, who suffered from asthma and worried that he might not get enough air in the shaft, stood guard at the top. At the bottom of the shaft, the others found a large, illicit coal mine, then heard shots and saw their rope—cut loose from the top of the shaft—drop to their feet. After several hours of scrambling up the shaft, the men emerged to find Walker lying dead of gunshot wounds. He was the first Secret Service agent killed in the line of duty.

The work of the Secret Service exposed large numbers of land frauds and regained millions of acres of land for the U.S. government. Later laws tightened the rules of homestead ownership.

By 1907, Congress decided that the Secret Service should no longer lend its agents to other government units. It then limited the work to the service's standard duties within the Treasury Department, including the protection of the president and, beginning in 1908, the president-elect. At this point, eight agents were transferred permanently to the Department of Justice, where they began the organization that eventually became the Federal Bureau of Investigation (FBI).

THE WHITE HOUSE'S OWN POLICE FORCE

Recognizing a need for more protection for the White House and its grounds, President Warren G. Harding requested a special police

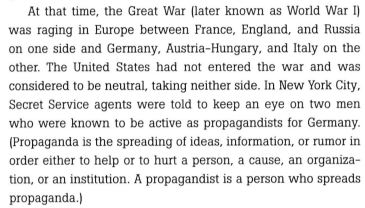

THE BRIEFCASE LEFT ON THE ELEVATED TRAIN

From time to time, the Secret Service has been asked to carry on investigations outside the parameters of its normal duties. One such instance was in 1915 when President Woodrow Wilson ordered Secretary of the Treasury William G. McAdoo to give Secret Service agents a special assignment.

At that time, the Great War (later known as World War I) was raging in Europe between France, England, and Russia on one side and Germany, Austria-Hungary, and Italy on the other. The United States had not entered the war and was considered to be neutral, taking neither side. In New York City, Secret Service agents were told to keep an eye on two men who were known to be active as propagandists for Germany. (Propaganda is the spreading of ideas, information, or rumor in order either to help or to hurt a person, a cause, an organization, or an institution. A propagandist is a person who spreads propaganda.)

On July 24, 1915, the agents were following the two, George Sylvester Viereck and Dr. Heinrich Albert. At 50th Street on the Sixth Avenue elevated railroad, which was like a city subway but was mounted on tracks above the street instead of running underground, Dr. Albert got up to leave the train. Agent Frank Burke, watching Albert, saw the

force in 1922, and by 1930 the Secret Service took over the force's supervision. Only 10 years later, White House police were on guard at Blair House (across Pennsylvania Avenue from the White House) while President Harry S. Truman lived there during extensive renovations of the White House. Puerto Rican nationalists, thinking they could assassinate Truman, tried to force their way into Blair House. In a brief skirmish, Secret Service Officer Leslie Coffelt was killed.

doctor leave behind a briefcase that he had been guarding closely. Burke grabbed it and left. Albert chased him. Burke got away.

The briefcase was delivered to Secretary McAdoo. Its contents revealed that German agents were working to sway American public opinion in Germany's favor by setting up news services and buying up newspapers. Germany was paying Viereck $1,500 a month to edit a publication called *The Fatherland*. And, the seized briefcase showed, Germany had plans to organize strikes in American factories that made munitions, get control of the supply of liquid chlorine (needed to make poison gas), seize the Wright Aeroplane Company and use its patents to build warplanes, and cut off England's supply of cotton and make it look as if Southern cotton growers in America had cut England off on their own.

There was more. Somehow, the papers disclosed, Germany had actually bought a large plant in Bridgeport, Connecticut, that made munitions. There it planned to receive orders from Russia and Great Britain for gun shells, but it intended to make no deliveries.

The facts about the briefcase papers were published, but the background on how the Secret Service got the briefcase was not revealed until 1931, when McAdoo published a book he had written called *Crowded Years*.

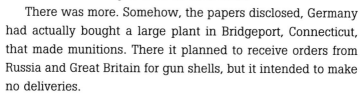

As a result of that attack, Congress permanently authorized Secret Service protection not only for the president but also for the president's immediate family, the president-elect, the vice president (or the next person in line to succeed the president), the vice-president-elect, and former presidents and their spouses. After the assassination of presidential candidate Robert F. Kennedy in 1968, Congress extended Secret Service protection to major presidential and vice presidential candidates and nominees. Over the next several years, visiting heads of foreign states or governments, widows of presidents, and the accompanying spouses of the heads of foreign countries were all granted Secret Service protection.

In the meantime, the White House Police Force was renamed twice. In 1970 it became the Executive Protective Service, and in 1977 it was officially titled the Secret Service Uniformed Division.

Recent years have brought added responsibilities. Laws passed in 1998 made identity theft and telemarketing fraud both criminal acts, and the Secret Service is responsible for investigating both. Three years later, after the USA PATRIOT Act put the Secret Service in charge of the investigation of fraudulent activity in connection with computers, electronic crimes task forces were established nationwide. And in 2002 the Department of Homeland Security was created, with the Secret Service transferred to it the next year from the Department of the Treasury. Over the next five years, the Secret Service made almost 29,000 arrests for financial crimes, including counterfeiting and computer fraud, with 98 percent of arrests resulting in convictions. In that period, it seized more than $295 million in counterfeit currency. In financial crime cases that resulted in convictions, victims suffered total actual losses amounting to $3.7 billion, while possible losses that were prevented by Secret Service action added up to more than $12 billion.

Protecting People and Places

It is springtime in London, England, and, unlike the usual April weather in Britain, the day is warm and sunny. At Winfield House, the home of the U.S. ambassador, shady magnolia trees are just coming into bloom alongside the lush green lawn—the size of several football fields—of one of London's largest private gardens. Inside, U.S. President Barack Obama, who has been meeting with world leaders during his first visit to Europe since taking office three months ago and who is known as a fresh-air enthusiast, has been frustrated because window coverings installed for security by the Secret Service prevent him from seeing the broad green spread. Now, his last guest having departed, he steps to a back door and looks out. "Come on," he says to his senior adviser David Axelrod and his press secretary, Robert Gibbs. "Let's go take a walk."

Secret Service agents jump into action, dashing ahead of the president. (A nearby Obama aide later said the agents "freaked.") Atop the building, snipers stand ready, carefully watching for some 45 minutes as the president and his aides stroll the broad lawn while discussing a current disagreement between representatives of China and France who will be meeting at coming talks.

Only two days later, in France, the president speaks of how hard it is to be spontaneous. "You know," he says, "it's very frustrating now. It used to be when I came to Europe that I could just wander down to a cafe, and sit and have some wine and watch people go by, and go into a little shop, and watch the sun go down. Now I'm in hotel rooms all the time and I have security around me all the time. And so just, you know, losing that ability to just take a walk, that is something that is frustrating."[1]

The president of the United States and the president's immediate family may be the first people who come to mind when thinking about whom the Secret Service protects, but the protection extends in a broad circle that includes the vice president and his family. Every four years, it includes the candidates of the major political parties who are running for president. They are protected for at least 120 days before the election. After the votes have been counted, protection continues for the president-elect and vice-president-elect and their families.

Former presidents and their spouses also get protection for 10 years after the dates when they leave office. So do their children if they are under 16 years old (or longer, if the new president issues an executive order to provide protection). Former President George W. Bush is the first who has his protection limited to 10 years. His predecessors, Presidents Johnson, Nixon, Ford, Carter, Reagan, George H.W. Bush, and Clinton, all received lifetime protection after leaving office, while earlier ex-presidents had none. As incoming President Dwight D. Eisenhower was inaugurated, for example, departing President Harry S. Truman and First Lady Bess Truman simply got into the family car and, unescorted, drove away from the White House headed for home in Independence, Missouri. In the past, former vice presidents have not been protected. Bush administration Vice President Dick Cheney, however, continued to get protection, on the orders of President Obama, for at least a year after he left office.

The Secret Service also protects some visitors to Washington. No, not your everyday tourists, but such special people as the heads of foreign governments and their spouses and other distinguished foreign visitors. In recent years visitors have included the following:

- Pope Benedict XVI, who in 2008 drew vast crowds to outdoor masses in Yankee Stadium in New York City and in Nationals Park in Washington, D.C., and visited major sites in both cities.
- President Felipe de Jesus Calderon of Mexico and Prime Minister Stephen Harper of Canada, who joined a North American Leaders Summit meeting in New Orleans, Louisiana, in 2008.
- Prime Minister Ehud Olmert of Israel, who participated in a conference of world leaders in Annapolis, Maryland, in 2007 to discuss peace in the Middle East.
- Presidents Hamid Karzai of Afghanistan and Asif Ali Zardari of Pakistan, who met in the White House with President Obama in May 2009 in response to President Obama's urging them to crack down on rising threats from Al Qaeda and the Taliban in both of their countries.
- President Ellen Johnson Sirleaf of the Republic of Liberia—Africa's first democratically elected female leader—as she delivered the commencement address at the University of Tampa in Florida in 2009.

American visitors to other countries are protected, too, if they are official representatives of the United States who are performing special missions abroad. Members of the president's cabinet, such as the Secretary of State, receive Secret Service protection wherever they go during their international travels.

HOW IT WORKS

Those who are permanently protected, such as the president, first lady, and family, have special agents permanently assigned to them. Members of this group come and go with the president wherever he appears. Foreign dignitaries, special visitors, and presidential candidates are protected by special agents assigned temporarily from Secret Service field offices. The words *special agent* identify a Secret Service employee whose work is the protection of people and their families in the government—or, on assignment, visitors from other governments. Among some 3,200 special agents, one out of nine is a woman.

Protection is not simply a matter of placing well-armed agents around the individual (or "protectee" in Secret Service terminology). It involves a wide range of planning, for the Secret Service's basic mission is to prevent an incident rather than fix something after it happens. That means a great deal of careful advance work, assessing and analyzing any threats or possible risks. Wherever the protectee is going, the Secret Service goes there first—whether simply to a Washington restaurant or to a high-level meeting on the other side of the globe. Teams of agents go to the planned destination and look it over carefully. They figure out just how much manpower will be needed to establish and maintain security at the site, what technical equipment will be called for, where the nearest hospitals are, and what the best routes are for safely getting the protectee away in case of an emergency.

Others are called on. Fire, police, and emergency medical service departments are alerted, all coordinated by an advance agent in charge. With them, the agent reviews intelligence information that agents have gathered, sets up checkpoints to help control access to secured areas, and outlines what various members of the team are to do in any emergency.

In effect, and in fact, the entire security operation becomes a network of law enforcement people and public safety people, including (depending on the size, duration, and complexity of the event) local, county, state, federal, and military personnel. All participants are kept in contact with each other through a Secret Service command post that acts as a communications center and monitors all protective activities.

The work does not end when the protectee departs. Afterward, agents review every phase of the operation, recording any unusual or unpredicted incidents and suggesting improvements for the future.

Closely related to all security operations is work that agents call "protective research." Agents and specialists examine information received from various sources, such as law enforcement or intelligence agencies, about individuals or groups who may pose a threat to a protectee. The information may originate from phone calls or from questionable e-mails or letters sent to the White House. This protective research is ongoing, 24 hours a day, seven days a week. Phone calls to the White House from people who expect or demand to speak to the president, for example, are intercepted by Secret Service agents. Depending on the nature of the call, agents may then do a complete security check on

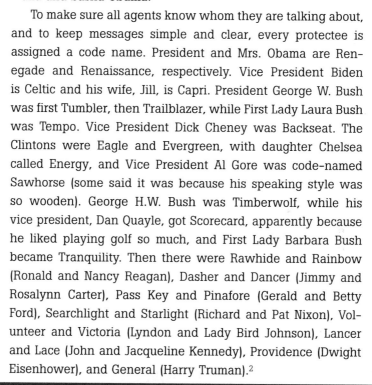

KEEPING UP WITH RENEGADE, RENAISSANCE, RADIANCE, AND ROSEBUD

What does it mean when a Secret Service agent's radio earpiece announces that Radiance and Rosebud are ready to go home from school? It means it is time to escort the president's daughters, for those are the Secret Service code names for Malia and Sasha Obama.

To make sure all agents know whom they are talking about, and to keep messages simple and clear, every protectee is assigned a code name. President and Mrs. Obama are Renegade and Renaissance, respectively. Vice President Biden is Celtic and his wife, Jill, is Capri. President George W. Bush was first Tumbler, then Trailblazer, while First Lady Laura Bush was Tempo. Vice President Dick Cheney was Backseat. The Clintons were Eagle and Evergreen, with daughter Chelsea called Energy, and Vice President Al Gore was code-named Sawhorse (some said it was because his speaking style was so wooden). George H.W. Bush was Timberwolf, while his vice president, Dan Quayle, got Scorecard, apparently because he liked playing golf so much, and First Lady Barbara Bush became Tranquility. Then there were Rawhide and Rainbow (Ronald and Nancy Reagan), Dasher and Dancer (Jimmy and Rosalynn Carter), Pass Key and Pinafore (Gerald and Betty Ford), Searchlight and Starlight (Richard and Pat Nixon), Volunteer and Victoria (Lyndon and Lady Bird Johnson), Lancer and Lace (John and Jacqueline Kennedy), Providence (Dwight Eisenhower), and General (Harry Truman).[2]

the individual to determine whether he or she is capable of harming the president or might seek an opportunity to do so. "If a threat is made against the President," says Secret Service deputy assistant director Richard Elias, "we want to know it. Whether it's a drunk in a bar or an identified terrorist, we're going to investigate it."[3]

AGENTS IN UNIFORM

Agents on permanent assignment to any protectee usually are dressed in civilian clothes, for two reasons. The first reason is not to alarm the public by appearing as a retinue of armed, uniformed guards. The second is to keep agents as undistinguishable as possible from ordinary passersby or members of the crowd that has gathered to see the protectee. (One can, of course, usually spot a male agent by his extremely close-cropped hair, his small gold-colored lapel pin, his full dark suit, his sunglasses—worn both to see better and so you cannot see which way he is looking—and the small coiled wire that runs down beneath his shirt collar from the radio earpiece stuck in his ear. The female agent is a little harder to notice.)

Agents on more general assignment to maintain security at the White House and other buildings are serving in the Uniformed Division. You can see them in uniform not only in the president's residence but also at the home of the vice president, in the U.S. Treasury Building and the Treasury Annex, and at the many foreign diplomatic missions in the Washington, D.C., area. They may also serve at foreign diplo-

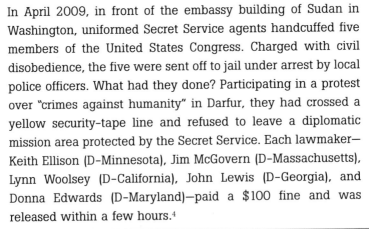

CONGRESS MEMBERS ARRESTED AT PROTECTED EMBASSY

In April 2009, in front of the embassy building of Sudan in Washington, uniformed Secret Service agents handcuffed five members of the United States Congress. Charged with civil disobedience, the five were sent off to jail under arrest by local police officers. What had they done? Participating in a protest over "crimes against humanity" in Darfur, they had crossed a yellow security-tape line and refused to leave a diplomatic mission area protected by the Secret Service. Each lawmaker— Keith Ellison (D-Minnesota), Jim McGovern (D-Massachusetts), Lynn Woolsey (D-California), John Lewis (D-Georgia), and Donna Edwards (D-Maryland)—paid a $100 fine and was released within a few hours.[4]

matic offices in other parts of the country if the president orders them to do so. They occupy a network of fixed posts and also patrol on foot, on bicycles and motorcycles, and in cars. This division, with 1,315 members, includes one woman for every nine men.

The Uniformed Division includes four groups of highly specialized experts.

- **The Countersniper Support Unit.** Members of this team are sharpshooters. You may see them on the ground or on rooftops. Their job is to defend the protectee against any medium- or long-distance threat. Their work demands perfect eyesight, tight elastic reflexes, and keen judgment.

(Continues on page 36)

A Secret Service Countersniper Support Unit watches an area where a helicopter carrying President Barack Obama will land in Cape Coast, Ghana, in July 2009. *(Shawn Thew/epa/Corbis)*

WHAT NOT TO TAKE TO A SPEECH BY THE VICE PRESIDENT

Shuyuan Mary Ho, a native of Taiwan, was a graduate student at Syracuse University. A few weeks before she was to receive her Ph.D. in information science and technology at the commencement exercises, she was surprised to receive an e-mail from the university. It asked her permission for the Secret Service to do a background check on her. Why? Because Vice President Joe Biden was to be the keynote speaker and she and 139 other doctoral students would be sitting on the stage with him.

An audience of 28,000, mostly relatives, was expected to attend the graduation of 5,018 students, but only the 140 assigned to on-stage seats would need to have the background checks. The entire crowd, however, could get to their seats only by passing through magnetometer checkpoints at each of several gates. That was the first of a number of rules that had to be understood by Shuyuan Mary Ho, her 139 associates who planned to be seated with her near the vice president, and all the rest of the large crowd. The rules, which are S.O.P. (standard operating procedure) when the Secret Service is in charge at any such event, were made public several days ahead of time by Timothy Kirk, the agent in charge of the Secret Service office in Syracuse. He advised those graduating to tell their invited relatives not to arrive with any large bags—backpacks, large shopping bags, or duffel bags—and to be ready for purses, camera cases, and binocular cases to be opened and inspected. His warning included the obvious: no firearms or explosive fireworks. But he also itemized a long list of things that would not be allowed in, including signs larger than two feet high and 18 inches wide, tape recorders, pocket tools such as Swiss Army knives, animals, laser pointers, noisemakers, coolers and food or beverages (unless for infants or for medical reasons), confetti, banners, balls, balloons, and air horns. In addition, he made it clear that no trash cans would be available outside the building, because trash cans are notorious hiding places for bombs.

Agent Kirk noted that the Secret Service had been working closely with the Syracuse Police Department, the Onondaga County Sheriff's Office, the New York State Police, and the university police, and that all officers working the graduation had had extra training. "We do set up a plan and program that enable the public to be accommodated," he said. "We don't restrict them. They'll be able to get through safely. This way, we can secure their safety as well as the vice president's."

The agent urged all those invited to arrive early. "We expect more people to show up, that's O.K.," he said, "but people need to understand that they need to come early if they want to be comfortable."

What did Agent Kirk *not* tell the public or the students who would be sitting on the stage with the vice president? Among other things, that an advance team of agents had gone to work weeks earlier surveying the huge building where the commencement exercises would be held, that they had anticipated every step of Mr. Biden's trip to Syracuse and planned every move he would make from the airport to the building and its stage, that they had checked on whether any arm of local law enforcement had reported any uniforms stolen, that they had determined the shortest route to University Hospital from any point on the vice president's tour, that the hospital's landing pad was not strong enough to support the Secret Service's heavy military Black Hawk helicopter but an alternative landing place was planned, that the hospital's emergency room was on alert to supply sterile "bunnysuits" to cover eight Secret Service agents from collar to toe and then find space for the agents in the operating room, that one or more of the people sitting on the stage in cap and gown would be neither student nor faculty member but, rather, one or more Secret Service agents.[5]

(Continued from page 33)

- **The Canine Explosives Detection Unit**. The skilled four-legged members of this team—all experts at sniffing out explosives— and their handlers check out areas that a protectee plans to visit.
- **The Emergency Response Team**. If anyone tries to intrude unlawfully into the White House or onto its grounds, these agents act fast. In tough, well-trained physical condition, they maintain an extremely high level of competence.
- **Magnetometer Support Unit**. To make sure that no one who is carrying a weapon is able to enter an area that is made secure for a protectee, agents on duty in this unit set up metal detectors at each entry point. Uniformed agents stand guard at each magnetometer, whether indoors or out.

WHAT MAKES AN AGENT?

A Secret Service agent guarding a protectee doesn't have to be bigger or stronger than other people. An agent does have to have instant reflexes and skills so ingrained that the agent is ready for combat in a split second. Emotions have to be under absolute control. Thinking has to be quick but careful, able to respond instantly to the unexpected. The agent develops, and maintains through ongoing training, a "sixth sense" about what is normal in any situation. Altogether, the skills that agents have learned, tuned up by repeated intensive training, make them

"THE SHIFT"

Several hundred special agents get to serve on the Presidential Protection Detail (PPD). How does one get that special duty? An agent may apply for it after five to seven years on the job. At any one time, five to seven special agents—called "the shift"—from the PPD surround the President. Twenty-four hours a day, these agents maintain a security "bubble" in all directions around the country's chief executive. As needed, they include rooftop snipers, bomb-sniffing dogs, and helicopters overhead.[6]

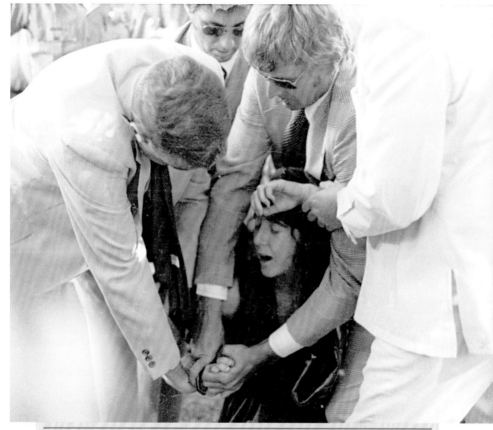

Secret Service agents put handcuffs on Lynette Fromme after she pointed a gun at President Gerald Ford as he walked from his hotel to the State Capitol building in Sacramento, California, on September 5, 1975. The agent holding Fromme at center, wearing dark glasses, is Larry Buendorf. *(AP Photo/Ron Edmonds)*

capable of reacting instantly and automatically to a threat without even thinking about it. It is what one agent calls "muscle memory."

A good example of an agent's work is what Agent Larry Buendorf did in Sacramento, California, on September 5, 1975. There President Gerald Ford, with Agent Buendorf right beside him, was shaking hands as he moved alongside a crowd. The agent noticed that one person in the crowd, a young woman wearing a bright red dress, kept pace with the president's moves. "All of a sudden," Buendorf said later, "I see a hand coming up, very slowly, with an object in it."

(Continues on page 41)

GETTING THE PRESIDENT FROM HERE TO THERE

On the morning of his inauguration, President Obama was ready to go to a 9:00 A.M. church service three blocks from Blair House, where he and his family had stayed the last few days. He intended to walk the short distance, but since 7:45 A.M. the Secret Service's 20 agents on duty had been organizing a 14-car motorcade. The president stepped out of Blair House's back door through 10 feet of fresh open air and into a new limousine built for him by General Motors. The trip, which included an escort of motorcycle police, took 90 seconds.

The car in which the president travels is different from earlier presidential limos in dozens of ways. Before President Kennedy was assassinated, they were designed as open cars so the president could be seen. Since then, they have been designed so the president can be protected. President Obama's limousine, known to the Secret Service as "The Beast," has armor-plated doors that are eight inches thick—as thick as the doors on a Boeing 757 passenger jet. Bomb blasts, rocket firings, and high-powered gunfire cannot pierce its armor plating. Its gas tank is not only armor-plated but also contains a special foam filler that will prevent an explosion if the tank takes a hit. The car is equipped with tear-gas cannons, pump-action shotguns, rocket-propelled grenades, night-vision cameras, and Kevlar-reinforced tires that, according to experts, cannot be punctured or shredded (other experts say the car can be driven at 60 miles per hour with punctured tires). It can generate its own oxygen supply and it is sealed against chemical attacks. Its windows, which can deflect armor-piercing bullets, do not open (except the driver's, which opens only three inches). A clear, bulletproof partition between the front and rear seats can be lowered only by the president. The car carries fire-fighting equipment, a state-of-the-art communications system that includes video terminals, and bottles of the president's AB blood type.[7]

The car described here is not the only one. A small fleet of identical, interchangeable cars is maintained, for two reasons. The first reason is to ensure that a car can always be ready wherever the president is. The second is so that wherever the president goes, "decoy" cars go, too, so no one (except those directly involved) knows which car actually contains the president.

The president seldom travels by train, but when he does the entire Amtrak railway system can be affected. On Saturday, January 17, 2009, three days before his inauguration, Mr. Obama journeyed by rail from Philadelphia to Washington as a salute to the nation that had elected him. Long-time Secret Service rules about presidential trains took effect. No electric locomotives were permitted, because they depend on overhead

(continues)

United States Air Force crew secure two presidential limousines inside a C5 military transport plane. A secure package of motorcade vehicles, including the limousines and a fleet of Secret Service SUVs, is transported to the site of every presidential visit. *(Brooks Kraft/Corbis)*

(continued)

wires, which are the standard source of power on that route. Rather, diesel engines had to be used, so the train could always be under its own power. And that meant two engines up front, in case one failed. In addition, an advance train, also with two diesel engines, ran ahead to make sure the rails were clear. And behind the president's train ran another, also with two diesel engines, to protect from the rear. In addition, two other locomotives were held in reserve. That meant a total of eight diesel locomotives that had to be cleaned and put in top running condition before the planned date. Where did they come from? Already short of enough locomotives to maintain regular service, Amtrak had to change or cancel service as far west as Chicago, in some cases for several days in a row, in order to provide the eight diesels that the Secret Service required.[8]

To go places that are not close enough to reach by car or train, the president usually flies in an Air Force jet or a Marine Corps helicopter. The Air Force maintains two matching Boeing 747-200B planes (each officially called "Air Force One" only when the president is aboard). Capable of refueling in flight, they have unlimited range. Each provides the president a large office and conference room, lavatory, bedroom, and gym. Quarters are included for Secret Service agents, journalists, senior advisors, and guests. A medical suite is ready for use as an operating room, and a doctor is always aboard if the president is aboard. Two galleys are stocked ready to feed as many as 100 passengers at a time. Advanced communications equipment enables the plane to serve as a moving command center if an attack on the United States occurs while the plane is in the air.[9]

Marine One is the official name applied when the president is aboard any one of several helicopters. They are used mostly to move the president quickly between any airport where Air Force One can land and any place where the president is visiting.

While the president's limo is driven by a Secret Service agent, Air Force One and Marine One, of course, are flown by pilots who are officers in those military services.

An unidentified Secret Service agent, automatic weapon drawn, yells orders after shots were fired at President Ronald Reagan on March 30, 1981, outside a Washington, D.C., hotel. *(AP Photo/Ron Edmonds)*

(Continued from page 37)

Instantly, without stopping to think or guess what the woman was doing, the agent jumped in front of the president, pulling the object from her hand and pushing her away from the president. "The minute I did that," he said, "I knew it was a gun." At the same time, other agents, reacting in a split second, covered the president and moved him away. "This is what we are trained to do," an agent commented afterward. "The moves become automatic."

Special Agent Tim McCarthy reacted instantly on March 30, 1981, when he heard gunfire as President Ronald Reagan was stepping toward his limousine from the door of a Washington hotel. Jumping in front of the president, McCarthy was shot in the stomach. Other agents pushed Reagan into his car. They zoomed off toward the White House as Agent

Jerry Parr checked the president for a wound but found none. Then he saw the president wipe bright red, foamy blood from his mouth. Immediately, Parr knew from his training that the president had been shot in or near his lungs. He ordered the driver to race to nearby Georgetown Hospital, which was only three minutes away. That quick reaction probably saved Reagan's life.[10]

THE BITTER LESSON OF NOVEMBER 22ND, 1963

Why does the Secret Service insist so strongly on training its agents to have immediate, instinctive, "sixth-sense" reactions? Why does it demand the opportunity to do protective research before any event at which it must guard a protectee? The answers to these questions lie in a bitter lesson learned the only time the agency failed to protect the life of a president—that of John Fitzgerald Kennedy on November 22, 1963, a day that, in a sense, continues to haunt the Secret Service.

A brief review of some key factors that went wrong that day and the days leading up to it can help to show why current agents do not accept the already-prepared plans of a protectee. Rather, they insist on participating in the planning from the moment an event is conceived.

In June 1963 President Kennedy, Vice President Lyndon Johnson, and Texas Governor John Connally began planning a Dallas trip as a political event to bolster Democratic voting in the forthcoming 1964 election. Early in October, Connally visited the White House to plan a motorcade and luncheon. In a press conference on November 1, he announced Kennedy's plan to visit Dallas, but not until November 4 was the Secret Service officially told about the planned trip. By then the luncheon site had been selected—before the Secret Service could review it for security. And by then the motorcade route had been chosen— without the Secret Service having a chance to warn that it would take the president past the tall Texas Book Depository and other high-rise buildings and around a tight dog-leg turn that would slow the procession almost to a crawl. Furthermore, on November 19, Dallas newspapers published the precise route.

On November 22 the Book Depository, from which the fatal shots were fired by Lee Harvey Oswald, had not been scouted or secured by

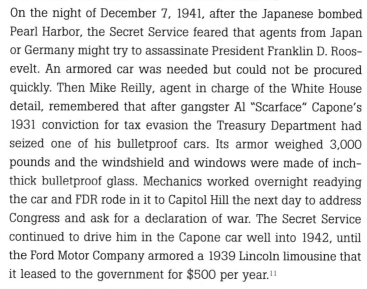

FDR IN AL CAPONE'S CADILLAC

On the night of December 7, 1941, after the Japanese bombed Pearl Harbor, the Secret Service feared that agents from Japan or Germany might try to assassinate President Franklin D. Roosevelt. An armored car was needed but could not be procured quickly. Then Mike Reilly, agent in charge of the White House detail, remembered that after gangster Al "Scarface" Capone's 1931 conviction for tax evasion the Treasury Department had seized one of his bulletproof cars. Its armor weighed 3,000 pounds and the windshield and windows were made of inch-thick bulletproof glass. Mechanics worked overnight readying the car and FDR rode in it to Capitol Hill the next day to address Congress and ask for a declaration of war. The Secret Service continued to drive him in the Capone car well into 1942, until the Ford Motor Company armored a 1939 Lincoln limousine that it leased to the government for $500 per year.[11]

the Secret Service. The tight, 120-degree hairpin turn in front of the Book Depository forced the driver of the Kennedy car, Agent William Greer, to slow down from the usual 20 to 30 miles per hour to only 11.2 miles per hour. Moreover, to give the eager crowd a chance to enjoy the sight of the presidential group, he did not resume speed after making the tight turn. Then came gunfire from high overhead. Agent Roy Kellerman, riding beside driver Greer, heard Kennedy say, "My God, I'm hit." Greer later said he thought he heard a motorcycle backfire. He had not had any special training in evasive driving. He knew he was not supposed to step on the gas unless Kellerman ordered him to. Actually slowing the car even more, he turned to look over his shoulder at the president. Kennedy's hands were at his throat. Greer turned back, then looked again. Six to seven seconds had passed. Now a second shot struck the president in the head. Only then did Kellerman say, "Let's get out of here, we're hit!"

Would Kennedy's life have been saved if Greer had recognized gunfire and instinctively sped away the instant he heard a shot?

President John F. Kennedy and Jacqueline Kennedy smile at the crowds lining their motorcade route in Dallas, Texas, on November 22, 1963. Secret Service Agent William Greer is driving Kennedy's car, with Agent Roy Kellerman riding beside him. Minutes later, the president was assassinated as his car passed through Dealey Plaza. *(Associated Press)*

What if Kellerman had not waited six to seven seconds to react after he heard the president say, "My God, I'm hit"? No one will ever know for sure, but Secret Service agents have been reliving those precious seconds ever since. And evasive driving and the recognition of the sound of gunfire have become key parts of agents' standard training.[12]

Investigating
Counterfeiting
and Fraud

At a Sonic Drive-In fast-food restaurant in Splendora, Texas, near Houston, a man presents a $20 bill to pay for supper for himself and a friend. With the store clerk nearby, the customer boasts to his companion about using fake bills to buy a car, and then jokes that he has to "go and make some money." The clerk examines the $20 bill he was just handed, and then shows it to the store manager. The manager calls the Splendora police.

A Splendora police officer arrives shortly afterward and finds the Sonic customer buying gas at a nearby Citgo station. In his car are $20, $10, and $5 bills that look phony. From his pocket the customer takes a wad of $20 bills. Police Captain Mark Seals finds that all the $20 bills have the same serial number. He places the suspect under arrest. His name is Tony Shawn McRee, and he lives in Cleveland, Texas, a few miles north of Splendora on Route 59.

Captain Seals knows the standard procedure. He calls the Secret Service. Agent Alberto Trevino responds, going to U.S. Magistrate Judge Frances Stacy to get a warrant for forensic examination of McRee's at-home computer. With the warrant, Agent Trevino, Captain Seals, and members of the Montgomery

County Sheriff's office go to McRee's home, where family members tell them that McRee recently bought a new Compaq Presario computer and led them to it. It is already turned on, with a program open. On the screen is the image of a scanned $1 bill. On the printer are uncut sheets of counterfeit bills. The investigators seize the computer.

They also find evidence that leads them to the Houston home of McRee's Sonic Drive-In companion, Shannon Ray Boudreaux. There, Secret Service agents and Houston police officers find scanners, printers, stolen credit cards, and a stolen BMW automobile. Now the Montgomery County Auto Theft Task Force takes charge of recovering the car.

Bringing charges, Agent Trevino files an affidavit that states that he believes the McRee computer contains evidence related to violations of Title 18, Section 471 of the United States Code (Obligations or Securities of the United States) and Title 18, Section 474 (Plates, Stones, or Analog Digital, or Electronic Images for Counterfeit Obligations or Securities). Both men are charged with third-degree felonies related to the counterfeit bills.[1]

The printing of what we commonly call "folding money" is not the only counterfeiting crime the Secret Service constantly faces. Criminals also work at creating counterfeit U.S. coins. They try to create checks like those issued by the U.S. Treasury, such as tax refunds. They produce phony food stamps that look like those issued by the Supplemental Nutrition Assistance Program (SNAP), formerly called the federal Food Stamp Program. Some expert artisans even create fake U.S. postage stamps.

TEMPTINGLY EASY TO DO

Up-to-date technology has made it possible for any dishonest person to yield to the temptation to try counterfeiting. The personal computer, combined with digital printing and photography, make it relatively simple. In fact, 61 percent of the counterfeit currency circulated in the United States from October 2007 to August 2008 was made using digital printing. In that period, the Secret Service arrested nearly 2,500 people worldwide on charges of counterfeiting, and it helped take out of circulation more than $103 million in counterfeit U.S. currency.[2] It should be noted, however, that the total amount of U.S. currency in circulation is approximately $829 billion—more than half of which is held outside the United States.[3] Proportionately, $103 million is a very, very small percentage of that $829 billion total.

The basic goal of the Secret Service's continuing investigation of counterfeiting is to cut down on the overall effect that this illegal activity has on the U.S. economy. The agency works jointly both at home in the United States and abroad with partners in international law enforcement to find out who makes counterfeit U.S. money and where they make it.

KNOW YOUR MONEY

Every Special Agent is well trained in recognizing counterfeit money. In Washington, D.C., at the U.S. Bureau of Printing and Engraving, where money is printed, agents learn the many characteristics of paper money—for example, the three distinctive colors of the serial numbers and the Treasury seal, the slight variations of detail that can be seen in reissues of some portraits on the faces of bills (some $20

A counterfeit quarter (left) is shown next to a real quarter. Counterfeit coins usually exhibit blemishes not found on genuine coins. (AP Photo/Wasau Daily Herald, Rob Orcutt)

bills, for instance, have Andrew Jackson's hand showing two fingers, while others show one finger), or variations of design in the official Federal Reserve system seal. As new bills are made to replace worn-out bills (a typical bill lasts only five to seven years), features that are progressively sophisticated are added to improve security and make them harder to mimic. Agents, of course, have to keep up to date on such changes.

NOT MADE IN USA

Early in the 21st century, Secret Service agents investigating the source of counterfeit American dollars found that many were coming from South America. Concentrating on Colombia, they set up an effort with that country to target counterfeiting operations large and small. This planned partnership is called Project Colombia. It provides training and develops strategies to help Colombian authorities. Over the project's first decade, the partners arrested some 600 suspects, seized about $221 million in counterfeit U.S. money, and put a stop to 75 printing plants that were producing the dollars. The result is a 75 percent drop in the amount of fake U.S. currency that comes from Colombia and is passed within the United States.

Following are two examples of this work by the Secret Service liaison office, called the Bogota Resident Office:

★ On October 24, 2007, agents working with Colombia's Vetted Anti-Counterfeiting Forces (VACF) raided a hotel room in Cali, seizing some $226,000 in counterfeit $100 bills—officially called U.S. Federal Reserve Notes, a title that can be read across the top of the face of any folding money. They also confiscated lithographic plates used to print the front and back images of the $100 notes.

★ On March 5, 2008, again working in partnership with the VACF, agents arrested an individual who was a carrier, or transporter, of counterfeit Federal Reserve Notes. They confiscated more than $9.8 million worth of $100 bills.

At the same time, agents are kept up to date on the latest counterfeiting technologies. In effect, they have to know as much as, or more than, the counterfeiters know about copiers and printers as well as ink-jet and toner particle technology. They are also trained in the science of making the special papers on which currency is printed, so they recognize paper that is not correctly embedded with tiny red and blue fibers.

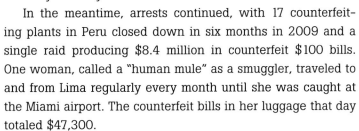

Following the crackdown in Colombia, the Secret Service noticed an increase in the production of counterfeit U.S. dollars in Peru. In 2008 agents seized more than $18.2 million in raids in that country, plus at least $7.8 million recovered within the United States but printed in Peru. "And that's just a fraction of the notes that we can ally to Peru" from around the world, said Assistant Special Agent John Large, who was in charge of the Secret Service's criminal division in Washington. "It's a form of economic terrorism." He said international counterfeiting reduces confidence in the U.S. dollar, which is acceptable currency in many South American countries.

In the meantime, arrests continued, with 17 counterfeiting plants in Peru closed down in six months in 2009 and a single raid producing $8.4 million in counterfeit $100 bills. One woman, called a "human mule" as a smuggler, traveled to and from Lima regularly every month until she was caught at the Miami airport. The counterfeit bills in her luggage that day totaled $47,300.

Some Federal Reserve Notes produced by counterfeiters in foreign lands are so well made that no one realizes they are phony until they reach the Federal Reserve Bank. The Secret Service has been finding and investigating these superior-quality notes since 1989. Agents report that the notes belong to a "family" of various versions of both $50 and $100 denominations. Their continuing investigation, which covers more than 130 countries, has resulted in nearly 200 arrests in the United States and overseas.[4]

Counterfeiters also attempt to produce acceptable coins. As with paper money, Special Agents are trained to recognize differences between genuine coins and fakes. Genuine coins are made by special machines that stamp them out (the experts say coins are "struck"). Counterfeit coins, however, are usually made by pouring molten metal into a mold. They are likely to show tiny—even microscopic—pimples or cracks.

How does an agent know whether the person passing a counterfeit bill has criminal intent or is the innocent victim of a counterfeiter? That may depend on the agent's skill at conducting an interview as well as strong background training in psychology. Tracking a bill to its origin is not easy. The agent begins with the neighborhood where someone—a store clerk, for example, or a bank teller—recognized the bill as phony. The agent tries to interview the person who passed it, and then works backward to find the source of the printing.

Whoever has accepted the bill and is holding it becomes the loser, no matter how much it is supposed to be worth, for turning in a counterfeit bill does not mean you get a real one in exchange. That is why small-time counterfeiters like to pass their bills, one by one, in busy places—fast-food restaurants at lunchtime, mom-and-pop stores, movie theaters just before the feature starts—when cashiers have little time to look closely.

A counterfeit bill is usually sent to the Secret Service laboratories. There, technicians use special chemicals to see if traces of human perspiration have left fingerprints, which may become forensic evidence if charges are brought against someone accused of printing the bill—or which may only trace some of the handling of the bill by innocent passers.

In many cases, the agents can find the path back to the origin of a supply of counterfeit bills by finding out how much the person caught with them paid for them. If the price was as much as 50 cents per dollar, it is likely there were several earlier steps going back to someone who paid the printer only ten cents for each dollar's worth. Agents also do preventive work to head off the successful passing of counterfeit money. Working undercover, Special Agents may create sting operations in which they buy large quantities of counterfeit money so they can get to where the bills originate, arrest the counterfeiters, and close down the entire operation.

FINANCIAL CRIMES

What is a financial crime? It is any dishonest method of getting money from a bank, a credit union, or any other financial establishment. It can involve only a few dollars or a large amount of money. Because United States currency is issued by the federal government, anyone accused of a financial crime is investigated by the Secret Service. Trials of the accused are held in U.S. district courts before U.S. district judges. If convicted by a jury and sentenced to serve time in prison, the accused person goes to a federal penitentiary.

Financial crimes are investigated by agents serving in 34 Secret Service Financial Crimes Task Forces (FCTFs) based in cities from New Haven, Connecticut, to San Diego, California. Interestingly, while there are five FCTFs in Florida, four in Texas, and others scattered across the country, there are none in the Pacific Northwest, none north of Omaha, Chicago, and Detroit, and none in such states as Arizona, New Mexico, New York, Pennsylvania, Maine, Vermont, New Hampshire, or Massachusetts. The task forces organize partnerships with local and state law enforcement agencies not only to look into suspected crimes but also to head off possible threats to any of our systems of financial payment. Among their jobs is the prosecution of financial criminals who commit such unsophisticated crimes as passing fraudulent checks and more complex crimes, including identity theft.

A FINANCIAL CRIMES TASK FORCE AT WORK

In April 2007 Secret Service Agent William Griffin of the Jacksonville, Florida, office was called by detective Len Schmauch of the nearby Brunswick, Georgia, police department. The detective said he wanted help checking into a complaint from Pastor Terrence B. Calloway of the New Life Community Church in Brunswick. More than $80,000 was missing, the pastor said, from the bank account of the church's Life Community Development Center. The money was supposed to be used to help pay for low-cost day care for underprivileged children, and included state as well as federal funds plus donations from church members. Because the money was missing, added the pastor, the center had been struggling financially. Its employees, mostly low-income single mothers, often could not cash their paychecks because the money was not in the church's bank account.

Agent Griffin went to work as lead investigator in the case. Carefully examining the development center's cancelled checks and its bookkeeping, he found that over more than a year—from May 2005 through July 2006—its director, Harriette Stafford Small, had apparently siphoned off a total of $100,209. The FCTF investigation revealed that Small had stolen most of the money by writing checks to herself. On other checks, she had forged the signature of her assistant, Cynthia Boggs. In addition, she had written checks on the church's bank account to cover her own personal bankruptcy, and she had paid herself double her actual salary.

Detective Schmauch and Agent Griffin arrested Harriette Small on April 23, 2007. She was then free on $10,000 bail while prosecutors prepared their case against her. Agent Griffin testified at her trial in March 2009. "When we sat down with Ms. Small and confronted her," he said under oath, "she admitted that she'd done it. She admitted that she'd forged Cynthia Boggs's name on the checks. Ms. Small also admitted writing checks out to herself."

Copies of forged checks that Agent Griffin had researched were introduced as evidence, while other evidence discovered during the task force investigation proved that the defendant had used the stolen money to pay for her $4,000 wedding and $1,000 honeymoon cruise to Jamaica with her husband and other family members. She had also spent thousands more on jewelry, clothing, and an automobile. Furthermore, $6,712 had gone to pay off her new husband's child-support debt. Other evidence showed that she had falsely claimed to have a master's degree in social work and that she had double-billed a previous employer for travel expenses.

The 11 women and one man on the jury, who had heard the defendant testify that Pastor Callaway had known what she was doing and had not objected, deliberated for 90 minutes on March 18, 2009. They then found her guilty on 27 charges of forging checks, bank fraud, and aggravated identity theft. She was sentenced on June 8, 2009, to five years in federal prison, plus five years probation and 100 hours of community service after completing her prison term. The sentence also included paying restitution for the entire amount stolen, as well as $2,700 in special assessments.[5]

Other typical investigations of financial crimes include the following:

- On December 16, 2008, a Long Island, New York, woman was accused of changing the face value of a stolen Social Security check worth $801. She etched a 6 onto the check, to make it appear to be worth $6,801, and then deposited it in her credit union account. A credit union fraud analyst called the Secret Service. The woman was charged with grand larceny and forgery.[6]
- Village police in Biscayne Park, Florida, called in the Secret Service when the town's finance director noticed unusual activity on its payroll account: It had mysteriously paid out more than $2,500 in a two-month period during July and August 2008. Investigating agents discovered that a group of five people were using a computer program that enabled them to download, design, and print their own checks. They created fraudulent checks that appeared to be from local businesses but that included the village's payroll account numbers. They then cashed the checks at check-cashing stores. They were careful to write no checks larger than $950 because they knew that a larger amount would trigger scrutiny by the check-cashing stores and by banks. The group members were charged with organized fraud, criminal conspiracy, grand theft, and criminal use of identification, and one was also charged as principal in the first degree for allegedly directing the group. [7]
- Agent Milagros McMaster filed a complaint in U.S. District Court in White Plains, New York, in February 2009, charging a certified public accountant (CPA) in nearby Chappaqua with stealing more than $223,000 from three of his clients. Over six years, the accountant had arranged for 37 of the clients' tax-refund checks to be sent to his home address. He then forged the clients' signatures and deposited the checks in his own bank account. Agent McMaster's complaint charged the accountant with mail fraud and forging endorsements on U.S. Treasury checks. In April, pleading guilty to one count of mail fraud and one count of forgery, the CPA admitted to stealing $300,000 in clients' tax refunds.[8]

ELECTRONIC CRIMES

Not long ago, electronic crimes were considered the crimes of the future. By the start of the 21st century, however, they had become a major factor in the world of law enforcement. To cope with the problem, the USA PATRIOT Act of 2001 ordered the Secret Service to set up task forces to "prevent, detect, and investigate various forms of electronic crimes, including potential terrorist attacks against critical infrastructure and financial payment systems."

At least 28 Secret Service Electronic Crimes Task Forces (ECTFs) have been established in cities across the country. They bring together experts from local, state, and federal law enforcement as well as from the academic and computer worlds to figure out cyberweaknesses before criminals take advantage of them. They have found that criminals use cybertechnology not only to communicate with each other but also to steal or extort money from victims and to hide evidence. And they continue to find that keeping up with the criminal mind is, as it has always been, a challenge in itself.

The many subjects investigated by the ECTFs include the following:

- Traffic in illegal firearms and narcotics
- Creation of false identification
- Creation of fraudulent credit cards
- Tampering with landline and cellular telephone service
- Threats against the president and other protectees

Agents are trained to recognize that a computer itself may have any of several identities: It may contain evidence of a crime, it may have been a tool in committing a crime, or it may itself have been stolen. The training must be continually updated so that agents are familiar with the latest in everything from mainframe computers to PCs and laptops and smartphones. They have to know how data—text or audio or images—can be destroyed or altered. They have to live with the fact that in the criminal world, as in the honest world, the technological learning curve never ends.

In Hoover, Alabama, the Secret Service maintains the National Computer Forensic Institute (NCFI), a unique school where local and state police officers as well as judges and prosecutors from anywhere in the nation—taking courses lasting from five days to five weeks—can learn how to investigate and analyze digital evidence.

Some typical crimes investigated by agents specializing in electronic crimes include the following:

- In December 2007 employees of a South Florida health insurance group manipulated the identification numbers of doctors and patients to bill Medicare fraudulently for more than $1.59 million.
- Also in December 2007, alerted by a major national bank, the ECTF in the metropolitan Washington, D.C., area identified a group that used information on the bank's customers to withdraw nearly $1 million. The group also set up an elaborate mortgage fraud system involving mortgage brokers, appraisers, builders, fake real estate buyers and sellers, loan processors, and escrow officers—all hooked up in a computer network and all adding up to a loss of more than $5.5 million.
- DirecTV was able to stop a fraud loss of more than $1 million in January 2008 when the Houston ECTF's investigation revealed that viewers who were not paying for DirecTV were altering satellite receivers and key cards to intercept TV programs sent from DirecTV's satellites.
- In Providence, Rhode Island, agents in January 2008 arrested two suspects for wire fraud and conspiracy, among other charges. The agents had found that an online electronics company had received payments from some 100 customers but rendered no services on purchase orders ranging from $77 to $2.3 million. The total fraud loss came to more than $14 million.
- In February 2009 a Secret Service investigation brought the arrest of three Florida men who were charged with hundreds of counts of credit card fraud. Creating fake gift cards in one of the largest violations of security in the history of bank credit cards, they had stolen data from Heartland Payment Systems, a New Jersey-based company that processes as many as 100 million transactions each month for banks across America. One business victim, the First National Bank of Omaha, which issues debit and credit cards nationwide, had to send out 400,000 replacement cards.

o Nineteen-year-old Dmitri Guzner of Verona, New Jersey, understood computers but did not understand that the U.S. Constitution guarantees freedom of religion. During one week in January 2008, denouncing religion, he and other members of an underground group called "Anonymous" hacked 488 times into Web sites of the Church of Scientology. By May 2009, as a result of an investigation by the Secret Service Electronic Crimes Task Force in Los Angeles, he was in U.S. District Court pleading guilty for his part in what cyberexperts call "distributed denial of service." He faced up to 10 years in prison and a fine of $250,000.[9]

INTERNATIONAL CYBERCRIMES

Cybercrime knows no boundaries and no state or national organization. It is as global as the Internet itself. Anyone engaged in cybercrime anywhere in the world routinely uses the same technologies that are a part of everyday life in the 21st century.

In mid-2009 the Secret Service announced the European Electronic Crime Task Force, a new unit charged with preventing computer hacking, identity theft, and other computer-based crime. Based in Rome, the unit pulls together the anti-cybercrime efforts of the U.S. Secret Service and the nations of the European Union. Leading the technology are an Italian anti-cybercrime police unit and Poste Italiane SpA—the Italian post office, which has moved beyond traditional mail delivery and developed software that can track electronic payments.

Among the task force's purposes is to monitor money transfers performed over computer networks across Europe, watching for such suspicious signs as an account being opened by the same person in several different places. Another goal is to bolster defenses against computer attacks on such sensitive computer systems as air-traffic control.

Announcing the collaboration, Special Agent Robert Gombar, in charge of the Secret Service's Rome field office, noted that countless Italians use Poste-Italiane's 14,000-branch post office as a bank for depositing paychecks and paying bills. The system earns more money from banking and insurance services than from sending packages and letters.[10]

On July 4, 2009, soon after the European Electronic Crime Task Force was announced, several U.S. government agencies began to find their Web sites knocked out. The sites of the Transportation Department, Federal Trade Commission, Treasury Department, and the Secret Service itself all were down at various times over the holiday weekend. Reporting the news on July 7, an Associated Press dispatch described it as "a widespread and unusually resilient computer attack" but said that government officials, who acknowledged that a cyberattack had occurred, refused to discuss any details. On England's BBC News, however, the announcement added that the Web site of the U.S. presidential office was slowed down or shut down for several hours. BBC also disclosed that at the same time some South Korean Web sites, including the presidential Blue House and Defense Ministry, were hit, with the implication that North Korea or its sympathizers might have been responsible for the attack. Two days later, as the media widely reported the cyberattacks, U.S. officials said they were unsophisticated and on a relatively small scale. A White House spokesman then admitted that its site had also been attacked.[11]

A week later, South Korean authorities reported that the cyberattacks used 86 IP (Internet Protocol) addresses in 16 countries, including the United States, Japan, and Guatemala, but added that it was uncertain whether North Korea was responsible.

IDENTITY THEFT

Who are you? How does a stranger know you're you? What happens if someone steals your identity and pretends to be you? How can you protect yourself from a thief who wants to take your personal information and use it?

These are the kinds of questions that arise when the subject is identity theft. It is a subject that is a particular focus of the Secret Service. And it is a kind of thievery that does not purposely target any specific individual. Rather, it finds its victims anywhere and everywhere, affecting all ages, races, nationalities, and genders. What the thief steals is data such as Social Security numbers, bank account numbers, credit card numbers, passwords—any information that can enable the thief to trespass into any kind of area that is supposed to be secure.

Some identity thieves utilize a routine known as "dumpster diving," in which they pore through trash looking for discarded receipts, bank

THE DUCT TAPE ON THE ATM

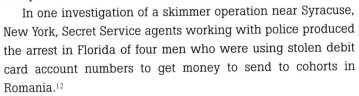

A man making a withdrawal from the Automatic Teller Machine (ATM) at his bank saw duct tape apparently holding in place the slot for his card. Later, when he discovered that a large amount had been pilfered from his account, he learned that an ingenious identity thief had stuck a skimmer into the ATM slot and used duct tape to hold it in place. The skimmer records data from the magnetic strip of any card pushed into it, giving the identity thief the information needed to create a fraudulent card. Some thieves even manage to place a small camera near the ATM to catch the Personal Identification Numbers (PINs) for the cards. "And I thought my bank was a bunch of cheapskates," remarked the victim, "using duct tape to repair their ATM."

In one investigation of a skimmer operation near Syracuse, New York, Secret Service agents working with police produced the arrest in Florida of four men who were using stolen debit card account numbers to get money to send to cohorts in Romania.[12]

Many news reports note that skimmers can be small enough to fit in an average pocket, making it easy for any dishonest worker in a restaurant or store to copy credit card data and sell it to a maker of counterfeit credit cards.

statements, or other reports that include key numbers. Others steal mail to find credit card and bank statements, preapproved credit offers, or tax information. Still others connect with someone who has a job that includes access to such information and who is willing to provide the information for a price. And others find a way or a connection that enables them to hack into a company's computers. The opportunities for identity theft are endless.

Usually the identity thief gets only the victim's number, not his or her name, but that is all the thief needs. The victim, meanwhile, is not aware of the theft until the arrival of a bank or credit card statement that shows a withdrawal or a purchase that the victim did not make. Then the victim has the tough, time-consuming job of repairing damage that may have been done to a savings account or a credit report—or even to the victim's reputation.

Some typical cases of identity theft that Secret Service agents and task forces have investigated include the following:

- A California woman working at a telephone answering service had access to the credit card numbers of customers. She was arrested in June 2009 for stealing some of their identities to buy more than $130,000 of merchandise and then selling it on eBay.
- A Texas woman working as a patient care assistant at a hospital was arrested in May 2009 for using patients' personal information to apply for credit cards without their consent. One of the patients had even died before the thief applied for the card.
- Over 18 months from October 2007 to March 2009, by getting Social Security numbers through his work as a mortgage broker, Californian Jerry Van Le stole the identities of some 25 children, immigrants, and others who had not yet established credit. He sold the numbers nationwide for anywhere from $3,500 to $6,000 each to about 2,400 individuals who used the numbers to establish fraudulent credit and make purchases totaling some $100 million. Le himself used the stolen numbers to get loans to buy a $500,000 home, expensive shoes and other clothing, several electronic and luxury items, and five vehicles.[13]
- Six waiters and waitresses were charged in March 2009 with stealing credit card numbers from customers at leading Washington, D.C.-area restaurants after bank customers complained of unauthorized charges on their cards. Investigating the charges, Special Agent Philip Soto found patterns that led him to the restaurants. Three men who bought the numbers from the servers had used them to create fake credit cards. The fraudulent cards then enabled them to buy gift cards and merchandise worth $750,000.[14]

Even the Secret Service itself can become the victim of identity theft. As reported in June 2007 on Wired News (a daily technology news Web site), Brett Shannon Johnson was an identity thief who specialized in stealing credit card numbers and filing fraudulent income tax returns. Over five years, he had stolen about $2 million. He was arrested in February 2005, and when he was freed on bond, agents in Columbia, South Carolina, who had been observing his activities for more than a year, offered to help him get a reduced sentence if he did undercover work for them. (Most law enforcement agencies use confidential informants to help their investigations.)

For 10 months, working in the Columbia office, Johnson infiltrated groups of credit card thieves on the Internet and informed the Secret Service on them. But at the same time, he continued to steal identities and use the stolen data to file fraudulent claims for income tax refunds—including data on taxpayers who had recently died but whose deaths had not yet been reported to Social Security. When the Secret Service caught on, it was paying him $350 a week as an informer, while his own identity theft scam, at which he worked in the office but mostly after hours, was paying him $5,000 to $6,000 a week.

"There were two agents with him at all times," Neal Dolan, special agent in charge of the agency's South Carolina division, commented later, "and we had a 42-inch plasma monitor that projected everything he did on it. You'd have to have been asleep not to have seen what he was doing, if he were committing crimes—and they weren't." He was investigated in March 2006 only because agents assumed that while he was away from the office and unsupervised he was warning one of their suspects. They gave him a lie-detector test, which he failed. Arrested, he worked out a plea agreement and pled guilty. In June 2007 a federal judge ordered him to serve six years and three months in prison and pay more than $300,000 in restitution.[15]

Secret Service agents can find themselves investigating fraud that takes advantage of the fair dealing and good faith of which our financial system is proud. Brian G. Parr, Special Agent in Charge of the New York Field Office, headed an inquiry into complaints of customers of Apogee Financial, Inc., that they had been defrauded of a total of more than $7 million. His team looked into a service that companies like Apogee perform in which they "lease" funds to a customer's bank account for a pre-determined period. The bank then gives the customer a Proof of Funds

(POF) letter that can be used to show creditworthiness in applying for a loan from some other lending institution. Agent Parr's group, reporting its investigation, filed a complaint in federal court. It said that Apogee gained customers by advertising its services, offering to lease funds in exchange for fees ranging from $40,000 to $750,000, but failed to provide any funds to its customers' bank accounts. Rather, in collusion with two employees of Wells Fargo Bank, Apogee printed fraudulent POF documents on bank stationery. Altogether, nine defendants—two bankers and seven Apogee employees—were charged with conspiracy to commit wire fraud because they advertised on craigslist.com.[16]

Anyone browsing the Internet in 2006 or 2007 could have stumbled upon CardersMarket, a Web site devoted to the theft of identities and credit card information that had some 4,500 members worldwide. A 16-month investigation by the Secret Service revealed that the site was maintained by Max Ray Vision, whose lawyer said he was a "hacker's hacker" who got into others' computers just "because he could." When agents raided Vision's California apartment, however, they found 1.8 million stolen credit card accounts with a total of $86.4 million in fraudulent purchases. Prosecuted in Pittsburgh, Pennsylvania, because two informants working there with the Secret Service had infiltrated his online operation, Vision pled guilty in June 2009 and went to jail in shackles to await sentencing. He is currently serving 13 years in federal prison.[17]

Recognizing
a Threat

In a Kentucky prison Scott Pennington is serving a life sentence. Two visitors come to see him. They say they have requested permission to interview him because they are conducting a special study of school violence. They know that several years ago Scott, a 17-year-old honor student in small-town Grayson, Kentucky, committed one of the first of our country's many school shootings. He killed his senior English teacher, Deanna McDavid, and a school custodian, Marvin Hicks.

The men introduce themselves. Bryan Vossekuil explains that he is a U.S. Secret Service agent who is the leader of the team doing the study. His formal title is director of the National Threat Assessment Center. The other man, Robert A. Fein, tells Scott he earned his Ph.D. as a psychologist. Getting acquainted, agent Vossekuil describes some of his extensive experiences when he traveled the world helping to protect President Ronald Reagan.

As they chat with Scott Pennington, Dr. Fein and Agent Vossekuil can tell that he is a bright, serious, and solemn man who is ready to answer any number of questions. They've asked the same questions, they tell him, of others who were responsible for school shootings—as many as a dozen or so. Among the many questions they ask are these: What were you trying to achieve? How did you choose your targets? Did you hope to be killed? How did you get your gun?

Pennington tells his visitors he had nothing against English teacher McDavid. He had shown her writings in his journals. He knew, he says, that she was concerned about them because they expressed thoughts about death again and again. He tells the men that he also knew that she told another teacher that she thought he would bring a gun to school some day and shoot either himself or somebody else. Not only that, he says, but she went to the school board and told them about her worry.

The men ask what the school board did.

They didn't do anything, says Scott. They told her it was up to his family to get him help.

The visitors ask if Scott can tell them just what his goal was.

It was to kill any two people, he says, so he would get the death penalty.[1]

The work of Agent Vossekuil and Dr. Fein was part of the program of the National Threat Assessment Center (NTAC), which the Secret Service created in 1998. Its purpose is to help Secret Service agents and others in public safety and law enforcement by providing guidance on how to handle threats. The basis for such guidance has four cornerstones: (1) research on threat assessment (that is, who makes threats, and what targets are likely); (2) training of law enforcement officials and others responsible for public safety on what to watch for and anticipate; (3) sharing of information among the agencies responsible for public safety and for protecting key people; and (4) programs that promote equal standards for all local, state, and federal assessment and investigation of threats. The overall purpose is to identify, assess, and manage those who have both the ability and the interest to attack public officials, other public figures, and people in schools.

VIOLENCE IN SCHOOLS

The interview with Scott Pennington was one of 10 that the agent and the psychologist held with people who had shot others in schools. It was part of a study that the Secret Service called the Safe School Initiative (SSI). Involving 41 students, the study looked into 37 incidents of attack going as far back as 1974, and it dug into school records, police records, and court documents. The idea was to try to find out what school shooters were thinking, how they behaved, and how they communicated their thoughts and attitudes before they made their attacks. The ultimate goal was to use such findings to help teachers, school principals, police, and others to notice or identify students who might be likely to commit violence.

Several key findings resulted from the study.

- First, almost all attacks were planned, not impulsive. Half of the shooters said they had thought about the shooting for at least two weeks and planned it for at least two days. In almost every case, someone else—another student, a teacher or school official, even a police officer—knew about unusual, disturbing behavior. In most of the shootings that were studied, in fact, one or more fellow students knew about the plan but kept it to themselves. For whatever reason, they didn't feel comfortable telling an adult. One friend of a shooter said afterward, "I was his friend. Calling someone would have been a betrayal. It just didn't seem right to tell."

- Second, no two shooters were alike, so the study could not draw any conclusions that would describe a profile of a typical school shooter. Most were not loners or people with histories of mental illness or alcohol or drug abuse, but more than half had felt severe depression or desperation, and three out of four either threatened or actually tried to commit suicide before the attack. One, Luke Woodham, had stabbed his mother to death, and then gone to his high school and shot nine students, killing two. He had written in his journal, "I am not insane. I am angry. I am not spoiled or lazy, for murder is not weak and slow-witted, murder is gutsy and daring. I killed because people like me are mistreated every day. I am malicious because I am miserable." Interviewed for the NTAC study, he said, "I didn't really see my life going on any further. I thought it was all over with. I couldn't find a reason not to do it."[2]

- Third, some school attacks may be preventable, and students can play important roles in preventing them. Before most attacks, other students knew what was going to happen. The study's inter-

An injured victim is carried out of Norris Hall on the Virginia Tech campus in Blacksburg, Virginia, on April 16, 2007. Seung-Hui Cho opened fire in a dorm and classroom, killing 32 people in the deadliest peacetime shooting in U.S. history. The Secret Service's Safe School Initiative was designed to prevent such incidents by providing information to police and school officials to help them manage potentially dangerous people or situations before they turn deadly. *(AP Photo/*The Roanoke Times, *Alan Kim)*

views with friends, siblings, and classmates (called "The Bystander Study") revealed that school shooters confided in them, letting them know their ideas and plans. Furthermore, other interviews showed that students who went to authorities with information actually prevented planned attacks from occurring.

By analyzing the studies, agents were able to develop useful information to help police and school professionals investigate and manage difficult situations and create safer atmospheres in schools. One particular goal since the studies has been to encourage students to tell responsible adults when they know about any possible threats to school safety.

Dr. Fein and Agent Vossekuil did not limit their studies to school shooters. In research called the Exceptional Case Study Project (ECSP), they interviewed the 83 people in the United States—at home, in hospitals, or in prisons—who between 1949 and 1995 came to be known as would-be assassins because they tried to attack or kill celebrities or public officials in 73 different incidents. The team's research found no stereotypes. Killers are not all male, nor are they isolated loners or lunatics. They make no threats, for, as several told the interviewers, if they voice threats they are likely to be stopped before they act.

Do assassins plan to kill because of hate? Only a few of the 83 said they hated their victims. Choosing a target was often an arbitrary decision. One woman who tried to get near the first President Bush with a gun said she "liked the man" and would have voted for him when he ran for re-election if she had not been in jail by then for threatening to kill him.

Or do they plan to kill just because they are violent people? The NTAC study changed Secret Service and police thinking about that. While they had always thought that a person either is or is not capable of violence, they learned from the study that violence depends on the circumstances. Killers often think about a plan for a long time but do nothing about it until some difficult event makes them desperate. Eric Harris, who with Dylan Klebold killed 12 students and a teacher at Columbine High School in Colorado in 1999, wrote his plans in a diary for a year. Then, wanting a military career like his father's, he tried to enlist in the U.S. Marine Corps and was rejected. He and Dylan committed the Columbine massacre one week later.

As a result of the study, the Secret Service recommends specific questions for police and schools when they are trying to figure out whether a person is dangerous. Among the questions: Has the person shown an interest in assassins, weapons, or militant groups? What has the person said about his or her intentions? Has the person been suicidal? If there is a history of mental illness, has the person acted on hallucinations or delusions?

Those who have worked with the Secret Service and been informed of the study have learned not to dismiss even vague reports of fear that come to them. "If someone's scared," said one Chief of Police, Anne P. Glavin, at the Massachusetts Institute of Technology, "we spend a lot of time trying to find out why they're scared."[3]

THE INSIDER THREAT STUDY

What happens if an insider—a worker, for instance, in a bank or in government—sets out to harm the information systems and data in his or her organization? The Secret Service's NTAC, in cooperation with the CERT Coordination Center of the Carnegie Mellon University Software Engineering Institute, made an extensive study of such possibilities. Its goal was to help those in law enforcement, government, and private business gain a better understanding of harmful insider activities. Why? Because an insider who has access to a computer system may be the most able to sabotage it. The study focused on identifying and analyzing the physical, social, and online behavior of current or former employees in order to see what kinds of behavior might be detected before an incident occurs. There are various reasons why an insider would want to harm an employer, including theft of intellectual property (that is, ideas), fraud, and sabotage.

The study explored four basic areas.

- **Insider threats to banking and financial institutions, including credit unions.** Here most incidents were not technically sophisticated. In incidents that were mostly well devised and planned, insiders, three out of four of whom were authorized users, entered simple commands. Generally the activity occurred during normal business hours and others knew of the insiders' plans, and many were directly involved in the planning or expected to benefit from the activity. The motivation? In 8 out of 10 cases, it was financial gain rather than a desire to hurt the system or the company. And the impact? In 30 percent of the cases, the financial loss was greater than $500,000.

- **Sabotage of computer systems.** Here the insider's main purpose was to sabotage the organization in some way or to harm a specific individual. Most such actions were triggered by some negative event related to work, with two out of three planned in advance and most done by remote access. More than half of the insiders knew how to take advantage of vulnerable applications or processes in their organizations' computer systems and were able to compromise computer accounts, create unauthorized backdoor accounts, or use shared accounts. Many of such activities brought financial losses, damaged organizations' reputations, or negatively affected business operations. Recommendations from the report included disabling computer access for any terminated employee, establishing a grievance process for complaints, creating ways for colleagues to report suspect behavior, setting up systems for detecting worms and viruses, and enforcing complex password policies.

NOT JUST FOR FATHERS CHECKING ON SONS

There is an old saying that crime is a growth industry. Two Texas brothers, Scott and Steven Wells, recognized that criminal activity on a computer is even more of a growth industry. They also knew that a Texas law passed in 2007 allows licensed professionals to gather private information and data from computers. So they took training courses and passed tests that awarded them Class A licenses in data forensics—that is, the tracking of data in order to assist law enforcement. They then opened a business that allowed them to utilize their computer networking skills, which were already well established, to help law enforcement people in dealing with computer crime.

Secret Service agents and other lawmen welcomed the brothers' partnership, called Wells IT Investigations, for it was the only service of its kind in central Texas and it met a big need: The load of cases was so great that it often took months before the kind of computer information needed for a specific case became available. "We can now alleviate the workload,"

○ **Illicit cyberactivity in information technology (IT) and tele-communications.** Sabotage, fraud, and the theft of intellectual property all occurred as illegal activities in the IT world. Insiders were able to affect various organizations, including Internet service providers, companies running e-businesses, makers and suppliers of software and hardware, newspapers, and consultants on IT and related services. The study found that insider activities were carried out by both current and former employees, with two-thirds of them holding technical positions, one-third with previous arrests, and the majority of insider activities planned in advance. More than half used rather sophisticated methods for their illegal actions, including scripts or programs, toolkits, creation of unauthorized backdoor accounts, and probing, scanning, flooding, or otherwise

said Scott, "process cases more quickly, and most importantly, help uphold one's Constitutional right to a speedy trial."

Someone asked Scott if a father could hire the firm to check on the computer activity of a teenage son. Scott said he could, but added, "We want to avoid the domestic cases. Our knowledge is to help catch criminals in criminal activities."

Describing the service the brothers provide, Scott explained a typical case—one, say, in which a computer has been seized by police and may hold valuable data evidence. Its hard drive, however, contains a dead system. It takes at least eight hours of work, he said, to get the data off that hard drive. Acquiring evidence from the data and then writing up a report add another four to eight hours. Thus a normal job involves 12 to 16 hours of labor.

Scott was asked about a concept that some computer users call "perceived anonymity"—the belief that something can be put on a MySpace page, for example, and that only friends will see it. That idea, he said, is foolish, for until the Internet goes away, whatever is put on it will be there for any devoted forensic specialist to take.[4]

compromising computer accounts. Most insiders were careful to conceal their activities and identities and were discovered only by failure of an information system or manual (nonautomated) detection of an irregularity.

o **Illicit cyberactivity in government.** The Insider Threat Study found that insiders in local, state, and federal government agencies committed sabotage, theft of intellectual property, or acts of financial or document fraud via computer. The majority of such insiders were employees with limited technical skills who worked in administrative and support positions. Nearly half showed inappropriate behavior before the incident, and more than half expected some financial gain. The method of 50 percent of the insiders was to take advantage of weaknesses in established processes or controls, such as procedures that were meant to keep duties separate but that were inadequate or poorly enforced, with the result that the insider was able to perpetrate such criminal acts as theft of intellectual property, document fraud, financial fraud, or sabotage by computer. Nine out of 10 insiders, in fact, had to face criminal charges, and most of them had not anticipated such consequences. The major effect on government agencies was damage to data or information. "In the end," the study's report concluded, "insiders jeopardized the public's trust in government agencies' abilities to protect citizens' personal and confidential information."[5]

OPERATION SAFE KIDS

Another kind of threat, the threat to the safety of children, is often a hidden one. If a child goes missing, his or her parents take immediate action. Usually their first step is to tell their local police department that the child is missing. And the first thing the police will do is ask questions about the child's vital information: height; weight; most recent photograph; fingerprints; distinctive information and characteristics such as hair color, eye color, scars, left-handedness or right-handedness, unusual speech impediments, names of siblings and other close relatives, and so on—whatever distinguishes that particular child from others.

Most parents do not have such information on hand, but many thousands of parents do indeed have it, for they have registered their children in a Secret Service program called Operation Safe Kids. It provides parents with documents that include biographical information, photographs, and digitized, inkless fingerprints. Such information saves valuable time, enabling those in charge to mass distribute the vital identification facts speedily to local, state, and federal law enforcement agencies.

To register kids, Secret Service staff (usually technicians from the Forensic Services Division) visit schools, boys and girls clubs, police departments, PTA events, and meetings of a wide variety of organizations to inform parents about the program and register children—all free of charge under the nationwide plan. The information is not, however, stored in any database. The document prepared by the Secret Service is for parents' or guardians' use only, to be stored at home or in any other safe place where it is ready for use if needed.

Operation Safe Kids is closely related to the Secret Service's partnership with the National Center for Missing and Exploited Children (NCMEC), an agency that has worked with the law enforcement community throughout the world since 1984. Secret Service technicians in all the agency's 138 field offices support the NCMEC through a wide range of services, including graphic arts and forensic photography, video production and the enhancement of both audio and images, voice identification, duplication of audio and video tapes, and the creation of three-dimensional computer models.

Handling Crowds and Major Events

"It's like knowing a snow storm is coming," says Kevin Evanto, "but not knowing if we're going to get five inches or three feet. You have several scenarios."

Kevin is a spokesman for Allegheny County Executive Dan Onoranto. The city of Pittsburgh, Pennsylvania, lies within the county and is getting ready for what is being called "The Pittsburgh Summit"—a two-day meeting of the leaders of 19 countries plus the European Union (also called "The G-20"). In cooperation with the Secret Service, Pittsburgh business leaders are making plans for when vehicular traffic is prohibited in downtown zones and buses cannot get to customary stops. "Downtown workers," says Michael Edwards, president of the Pittsburgh Downtown Partnership, "should be prepared to do some extra walking from remote bus stops or parking lots."

Secret Service Special Agent Malcolm Wiley coordinates meetings with more than a dozen planning committees. They deal with every topic from how to transport those attending the summit to how to train the police for control of expected demonstrators. "This is an effort to make sure all of the agencies are on the same page when discussing security preparations," he says. "We're *looking to provide accurate information." He reminds Pittsburgh officials and business leaders that the previous G-20 event, held in London, England, drew tens of thousands of demonstrators.*

While planning for security is going on, Pittsburgh's Thomas Merton Center, which focuses on issues of peace and social justice, applies for a permit from the city to march downtown during the summit. Along with 40 other groups, it is organizing a "permitted rally." City officials say they cannot approve any permits until the Secret Service announces the security boundaries for the event.[1]

The Secret Service's work on national special security events began in May 1998 when President Bill Clinton issued a directive that dictated what each federal agency was to do about security for such events. The purpose was to make responsibilities clear and to avoid duplicating resources and efforts. From that presidential directive came the term "National Special Security Events." A federal law, the Presidential Protection Act of 2000, made President Clinton's directive permanent, confirming the Secret Service as lead agency "in the planning, coordination, and implementation of security operations at special events of national significance."

The Secretary of Homeland Security decides if an event is big enough and significant enough to be designated a National Special Security Event (NSSE). Such events can take place anywhere in the United States.

As the planning begins, Secret Service agents line up partnerships with state and local police, fire departments, and medical emergency officials and workers, as well as others responsible for public safety and security. They plan a safe and secure environment not only for their protectees but also for visiting and local dignitaries, people participating in or watching the event, and the general public. This involves extensive planning. A motorcade is almost always part of the event, and that means scouting the entire route it will take and deciding where to assign rooftop security experts and how much traffic control will be needed. Countless details that must be considered include state-of-the-art communications so that everybody can talk to each other (on September 11, 2001, New Yorkers learned that the communications systems of their police officers and firefighters were not compatible). Checkpoints where credentials

AN APOLOGY FROM THE SECRET SERVICE CHIEF

Not everyone entitled to see the inauguration of President Barack Obama actually got to see the inauguration. Of the 1.8 million people who flocked to Washington, D.C., on January 20, 2009, several thousand held legitimate tickets marked with the colors purple or blue. These tickets entitled their holders to enter an area marked with those colors that could be reached by using the southbound Third Street tunnel under the National Mall. The Special Security Event plan was to keep the nearby northbound tunnel closed to the public and reserve it for use by emergency vehicles.

But a truck loaded with crowd-control barriers was vandalized on its way to the northbound tunnel and never arrived there. So no barriers kept thousands of people who held purple tickets from entering the northbound tunnel, not knowing that it did not lead to their planned viewing area. They were stuck in that tunnel for hours, shivering in the cold and missing the event for which many had traveled great distances at great expense. They called it "the purple tunnel of doom."

can be quickly and reliably approved or denied must be established, often with the capability of handling more than one foreign language. The plans include careful scheduling of the use of airspace where planes carrying key people will be coming and going. Canine teams figure out the best places to station their four-legged, bomb-sniffing experts. If the event is being held in any seacoast city, members of the U.S. Coast Guard join the team. Altogether, the task of every person planning any NSSE is to expect and be ready for someone to try to disrupt the event or endanger the security of a protectee.

The planning includes training even the most experienced law enforcement personnel in the special aspects of a major event. Because Secret Service agents train continually, they are ready to respond to any eventuality and to teach others how to respond. They simulate attacks

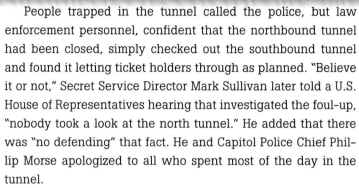

People trapped in the tunnel called the police, but law enforcement personnel, confident that the northbound tunnel had been closed, simply checked out the southbound tunnel and found it letting ticket holders through as planned. "Believe it or not," Secret Service Director Mark Sullivan later told a U.S. House of Representatives hearing that investigated the foul-up, "nobody took a look at the north tunnel." He added that there was "no defending" that fact. He and Capitol Police Chief Phillip Morse apologized to all who spent most of the day in the tunnel.

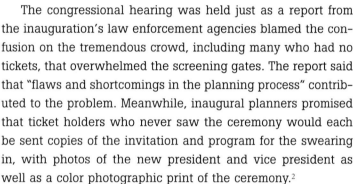

The congressional hearing was held just as a report from the inauguration's law enforcement agencies blamed the confusion on the tremendous crowd, including many who had no tickets, that overwhelmed the screening gates. The report said that "flaws and shortcomings in the planning process" contributed to the problem. Meanwhile, inaugural planners promised that ticket holders who never saw the ceremony would each be sent copies of the invitation and program for the swearing in, with photos of the new president and vice president as well as a color photographic print of the ceremony.[2]

and medical emergencies to help the NSSE team coordinate their specific skills. Both in the field (that is, out where the event is to occur) and in classroom-like sessions they develop mental and physical exercises that hone such skills. The purpose of the training is to make sure that everyone is ready to respond to any possible occurrence.

A VARIETY OF NSSEs

NSSEs range from professional football's annual Super Bowl to a visit to the United States by the pope, and from the Olympics in Utah to the G-8 Summit meeting of international leaders in Georgia. Following are some NSSEs that have been protected by Secret Service leadership in the 21st century (note that not all are political events and not all protectees are politicians):

- **The annual United Nations General Assembly.** Held each fall in New York City, this event brings as many as 116 foreign heads of state or government leaders, along with 58 spouses, who must be protected. Usually the U.S. president and any number of cabinet members, as well as senators and congressmen, also appear in the UN complex.

- **The International Monetary Fund (IMF) and the World Bank Group.** Every three years, these two groups meet each fall and spring in Washington for two consecutive years and in another member country in the third year. With the IMF considered a temporary foreign mission during the event, the Secret Service is in charge of security. Protectees include the U.S. secretary of the treasury and key foreign leaders.

- **The president's annual State of the Union address.** As our president presents the official report on our country's overall condition, the Secret Service is responsible for planning security in and around the U.S. Capitol and its chamber of the House of Representatives, as well as for protecting not only the president, vice president, and first lady but the cabinet members, Supreme Court justices, guests in the gallery, and senators and congressmen crowding the House floor as well.

- **Democratic and Republican National Conventions.** Held every four years, these NSSEs place extra-special demands on the Secret Service. Senior special agents take charge as coordinators of event security, pulling together extensive teams of local and state law enforcement officials as well as Federal Bureau of Investigation (FBI) and Federal Emergency Management Agency (FEMA) experts. They develop wide-ranging security plans, including assigning specialists who can identify and hold down any risks to cybersecurity, as well as training all team members in the use of the communications media that relay critical information during the convention. The total plan includes using the canine explosives detection teams of the Secret Service's Uniformed Division as well as its Countersniper and Counter Assault teams.

  At the 2008 Democratic National Convention in Denver, Colorado, agents and their team secured the Pepsi Center for four days, creating credentials for 18,000 public safety and law enforcement personnel and screening some 35,000 individuals each day. On the convention's final night, when Senator Obama accepted the nomination during an outdoor event at INVESCO Field, 80,000 spectators were screened.

A St. Paul, Minnesota, police officer mans the closed–circuit television command center at headquarters in August 2008 as security preparations for the Republican National Convention continue. Before National Special Security Events, senior Secret Service agents must develop extensive security plans and coordinate and direct personnel from local, state, and federal law enforcement agencies. *(AP Photo/Jim Mone)*

Members of the Secret Service opened the Denver Multi Agency Communications Command Center for a news media tour on August 22, 2008, in Denver, Colorado. The command center allowed all 62 federal and local agencies responsible for safety and security to monitor and record everything related to the Democratic National Convention. *(Getty Images)*

The 2008 Republican National Convention in Saint Paul, Minnesota, brought similar demands. The 19,000-seat Xcel Energy Center was secured for four days, with 6,500 credentials produced for law enforcement and public safety officials and 35,000 people screened daily. As at the Democratic convention, dogs sniffed for explosives, with sharp-eyed countersnipers and well-trained counter-assault teams ready if needed.

○ **The inauguration of the president**. This NSSE, which comes every four years, demands that the Secret Service work on a scale probably more vast than any other. Getting ready for the 2009 inauguration of President Obama, the agency set up 23 planning teams, coordinating the work of District of Columbia police as well as 4,000 additional officers from 96 other jurisdictions, 4,000 National Guard members, and 7,500 military troops including medical teams and experts in chemical attack. A command center run by the Secret Service and providing desks—each with two dozen telephone lines—for 100 officials was set up to begin operating on the Saturday before the Tuesday inauguration. Its TV monitors—equipped with live transmissions from such agencies as the Metropolitan Police Department, FBI, National Park Service, District of Columbia Transportation Department, National Geospatial-Intelligence Agency, and others—could show anything from current newscasts to street maps.

On Inauguration Day, a crowd estimated at nearly 2 million thronged the stretch of two miles from the west lawn of the U.S. Capitol to the Lincoln Memorial. This included 250,000 ticket holders seated before the Capitol. Spectators who came to the National Mall did not have to have tickets and could watch and hear the president's swearing in and inaugural speech on more

DID HE OR DID HE NOT WEAR IT?

A news report filed on the Internet the day after the inauguration of President Barack Obama said that, "according to some reports," the president "wore a suit made by a clothier specializing in bullet-resistant clothing" during the inauguration ceremonies. The report speculated that the suit might have been produced by a designer in Colombia named Miguel Caballero, who is noted for developing super-tough garments that are flexible and apt for business wear. His usual customers are Colombians and other Latin Americans who live amid violent conflict. His clothing is said to provide more than three levels of ballistic protection and is seven times more flexible than the usual Kevlar bulletproof vest. The secret is dense strands of Kevlar—some 500 to 1,500 filaments per strand of yarn—woven into the cloth.

Questioned about the suit, Secret Service officials said they could neither confirm nor deny the report.[3]

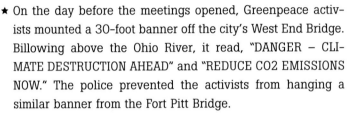

THANKS TO THOROUGH PLANNING

"Pittsburgh emerges from G-20 with hardly a scratch," said a headline after the event was over. Despite its invasion by several thousand aides and staffers on official business, plus 5,000 protesters and 6,000 miscellaneous law enforcement personnel, the city suffered no significant harm. Among noteworthy events were the following:

★ On the day before the meetings opened, Greenpeace activists mounted a 30-foot banner off the city's West End Bridge. Billowing above the Ohio River, it read, "DANGER – CLIMATE DESTRUCTION AHEAD" and "REDUCE CO2 EMISSIONS NOW." The police prevented the activists from hanging a similar banner from the Fort Pitt Bridge.

★ A federal judge ruled against two protest groups—the Seeds of Peace, which provides food and medical care to protest groups, and Three Rivers Climate Convergence, an organization that addresses connections and solutions to environmental and economic issues. After Pittsburgh police in body-armor riot gear and wielding semiautomatic weapons had stormed into and searched their headquarters, they had filed a suit claiming harassment against their "First Amendment activities." The judge said they suffered no "irreparable harm."

than 20 giant video screens. They were screened, however, at entry gates to the mall, and all were warned not to bring such items as thermoses, coolers, folding chairs, and umbrellas. Precautions included guarding against one or more suicide bombers or any troublemaker with a smoke bomb, which could cause disastrous results if spectators trampled others as they fled in panic. To help control the incoming flow of people, more than 60 bridges, highways, and local streets were closed except for official vehicles. Secret Service agents were assigned to survey every building along the Pennsylvania Avenue parade route, with snipers positioned on rooftops and balconies. Nondescript boxes that detect airborne

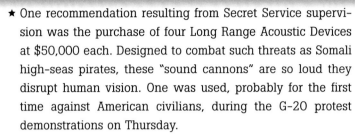
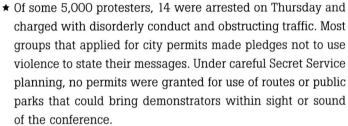
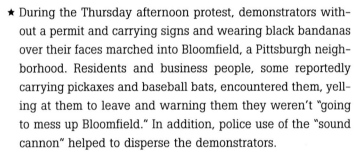

★ One recommendation resulting from Secret Service supervision was the purchase of four Long Range Acoustic Devices at $50,000 each. Designed to combat such threats as Somali high-seas pirates, these "sound cannons" are so loud they disrupt human vision. One was used, probably for the first time against American civilians, during the G-20 protest demonstrations on Thursday.

★ Of some 5,000 protesters, 14 were arrested on Thursday and charged with disorderly conduct and obstructing traffic. Most groups that applied for city permits made pledges not to use violence to state their messages. Under careful Secret Service planning, no permits were granted for use of routes or public parks that could bring demonstrators within sight or sound of the conference.

★ During the Thursday afternoon protest, demonstrators without a permit and carrying signs and wearing black bandanas over their faces marched into Bloomfield, a Pittsburgh neighborhood. Residents and business people, some reportedly carrying pickaxes and baseball bats, encountered them, yelling at them to leave and warning them they weren't "going to mess up Bloomfield." In addition, police use of the "sound cannon" helped to disperse the demonstrators.

releases of biological or chemical weapons were strategically placed. At least 5,000 portable toilets were also scattered around the grounds of the event, and enough parking for 10,000 charter buses was planned.[4]

o **The pope visits the United States.** In April 2008 Pope Benedict XVI spent six days in Washington, D.C., and New York City. As the lead law enforcement agency handling security, the Secret Service coordinated an extensive team of agents and local police, along with its other usual public safety professionals. Travel routes covered every move from Andrews Air Force Base outside Washington to the Manhattan site of the former World Trade Center. Two major sites were Nationals Park in Washington and Yankee Stadium in New York, where baseball diamonds served as the shrines where outdoor papal masses were celebrated. Altogether, 198,000 people were screened by some 500 Secret Service Uniformed Division officers using 127 magnetometers.

o **The September 2009 G-20 Summit in Pittsburgh.** This NSSE brought together the finance ministers and central bank governors of 19 nations plus the European Union, with delegations from another half dozen countries also in attendance. The meeting's purpose was to provide a forum for discussion by major developing and industrialized countries of key issues in the world economy. For James Gehr, special agent in charge of the Pittsburgh Secret Service office, the event called for planning to protect some 1,100 visitors from foreign lands. One of the countless problems that he and his team of metropolitan and state police had to face was the fact that almost any concert or sporting event usually backed up traffic in the city's downtown triangular street grid—and baseball's Pittsburgh Pirates had home games (one an afternoon start) scheduled on both days of the G-20. To cope with the possible blockage, several streets were closed. Because traffic restrictions could make it hard for students to get to and from schools, the Pittsburgh Public School system closed 66 schools and the Catholic Diocese of Pittsburgh closed four high schools and 13 elementary schools for two days. Augmenting the city's 877 policemen and women, more than 4,000 officers were borrowed from dozens of Pennsylvania cities, with additional help from Maryland, West Virginia, and New York state police. And to get extra advice on handling expected crowds of protestors, English riot police officers were imported from London. In that city in April, during the previous G-20, they had experienced all-day protests by a crowd estimated at 4,000 that had provoked bloody skirmishes and 32 arrests. To accommodate peaceful protests in Pittsburgh, permits were issued for a large rally of 8,000 to 10,000 people and six other protest-related activities, including a march downtown from the University of Pittsburgh and Carnegie Mellon University.[5]

What It Takes to Learn How

On his way to a dental appointment, Tom Potter has just parked his car, its window open, in a Maryland suburb. He opens the door to get out. From the car beside his, a shout stops him. "Watch that gun!" yells a man standing at the driver's door of the other car.

"It's not my gun!" a second man cries from inside the other car.

Potter slips back into his car and ducks down.

"Get out and keep your hands behind your back!" shouts the first man, pulling handcuffs from his pocket.

The other driver is quickly handcuffed. He and the first man now turn to Potter, who is frozen behind his car's steering wheel. "You're not part of this?" asks the first man.

Potter explains his dental appointment and hurries away.

The first man, who had the handcuffs, is a Secret Service trainee. The second is a professional actor hired to play a role in training sessions at the James J. Rowley Training Center near Washington, D.C. While most of their training exercises take place inside the center, some are "staged" in such remote areas as the parking lots of business buildings or in public parks or bus and subway stations. This gives both new agents and established officers in retraining a chance to experience, through role-playing, the emotional as well as physical sides of what they are studying in the classroom. Here, for example, the effect was so realistic that when Tom Potter parked beside the other two men they both assumed he was another actor participating in their training session. Needless to say, the exercise also fooled Potter, who did not recognize the situation as a training simulation.[1]

For a Secret Service special agent, training never ends. It begins with a one-week orientation course at the service's James J. Rowley Training Center in Beltsville, Maryland. After evaluation there, the new trainee attends a 12-week course at one of three Federal Law Enforcement Training Centers (FLETC)—in Glynco, Georgia; Charleston, South Carolina; or Artesia, New Mexico. Upon completing this course successfully (which not every student does), the trainee moves to a 16-week Special Agent Training Course at the Rowley Center.

12 WEEKS AT FLETC

In the federal course, the future Secret Service agent joins trainees from more than 80 federal agencies from across the United States and its territories. Together they gain a basic foundation of knowledge of investigative techniques and criminal law. This includes such specific activities as defensive tactics, the techniques of making an arrest, and the safe handling and proper use of firearms and other weapons.

The firearms training at FLETC is intense. Students shoot a .357-caliber semiautomatic pistol, aiming at a life-size, silhouette-shaped target marked with a 10-inch circle that has five rings that score from six to 10—the smallest only two inches in diameter but scoring 10 points. Proficiency on the practical pistol course must be 210 points out of 300 (70 percent). If a student fails, he or she must leave the program.

As they develop into sharpshooters, the trainees learn trigger control by practicing slow, timed, and rapid-fire shooting. They also learn to take their weapons apart, clean them, and put them back together.

Physical exercises to put the trainees in tip-top shape and keep them that way include pushups and pull-ups, 1.5-mile runs, and swimming. Nonswimmers soon learn to swim, and poor swimmers get special training to improve their skills in water safety. Before graduation, all are tested for flexibility, speed and agility, upper body strength, aero-

President George W. Bush *(background)* and a Secret Service instructor watch a Secret Service dog trainer and his dog check suitcases for explosives during a training exercise at the James J. Rowley Training Center in Beltsville, Maryland. *(Associated Press)*

bic capacity, and body composition—a measurement of skin fold to determine body fat. To earn a FLETC certificate, a trainee must score at least 70 percent in physical efficiency, but Secret Service trainees must achieve 80 percent.

KNOWING GUNS, CROWDS, AND CARS

After passing the FLETC course, the trainee moves to the Rowley Training Center for a 16-week Special Agent Training Course. Here the training is even more intensive and wide ranging than in the federal course, and it is designed to be stressful. It repeatedly subjects trainees

SEEN AND NOT SEEN

Some agents in the Uniformed Division get assigned to the Emergency Response Team (ERT). On duty, they are constantly alert, watching for any sign that someone is out of place or behaving in any way that seems suspicious. The work they do calls for a sharp mind, absolute control of emotions, and reflexes that spring into action in a split second.

Often the agents on ERT duty are in a now-you-see-them-now-you-don't mode. For example, when television shows the president striding across the White House lawn to board the Marine One helicopter for a trip, the well-kept shrubbery and trees in the background are visible. The ERT agents behind the trees or in the bushes are not visible, but they are there.

Special Agent Tim McCarthy's experience protecting President Ronald Reagan is a good example of an emergency response. He was alongside President Reagan as they stepped from a hotel in the nation's capital on March 30, 1981. Hearing a shot, he darted in front of the president. A second bullet hit McCarthy in the stomach. Two other agents pushed Reagan into his limousine and it dashed away. The total time that elapsed from the first shot to the limousine speeding away was perhaps 10 seconds.

Years earlier, in Dallas on November 23, 1963, Special Agent Rufus Youngblood's reflex action took over when he heard the shots that killed President John F. Kennedy. He instantly threw himself on top of Vice President Lyndon Johnson.

February 8, 2001, saw five shots fired at the White House from outside the fence along the South Lawn. Many tourists

to sudden, unexpected attacks that simulate real-world situations. Veteran agents, who return to Rowley regularly for refresher courses, get the same stressful surprises. Following are some of the areas of rigorous training that every agent must master:

ducked and ran. Others stood frozen in place. ERT agents surrounded a middle-aged man who held a gun. For 10 minutes
they tried to persuade him to release the gun. When he raised
it again, aiming toward the crowd, an ERT member shot him
in the leg. He was later diagnosed as mentally ill.

Secret Service Emergency Response Team officers patrol the south
lawn of the White House prior to President Barack Obama leaving for
a day trip to Columbus, Ohio, in March 2009. *(AP Photo/Ron Edmonds)*

- **Firearms.** Concentrating on protective work, the Rowley Center's
  firearms training is more complex than that at FLETC. Special
  agents must become familiar with a wide assortment of weapons
  and become well qualified to handle at least three: a shotgun, an

automatic weapon, and the .357-calilber pistol. They learn to shoot at moving as well as stationary targets, in daylight and in darkness. They practice shooting at targets moving across the firing range (called "running man" simulations) and shooting from inside moving vehicles as well as from behind parked cars.

○ **Control tactics.** Because protectees appear in crowded situations so often, training in crowd control gets a big share of the Rowley schedule. Trainees learn how to work a rope line—that is, the barrier (which may actually be a rope or a lineup of police sawhorses) between the protectee and the public when the protectee is greeting people and shaking hands. Trainees also must react instantly to a simulated, unexpected "AOP," or attack on the protectee, which their instructors may stage at any time. Training weapons fire blank cartridges called "simunition," which are small paint pellets that can break the skin, so trainees wear protective clothing.

○ **Driving.** Trainees who may have thought they were skillful drivers at age 16 learn very different ways to handle cars. They maneuver through obstacles at various speeds, slide on a skid-pan slick with water to learn how to control skids, and gain new respect for the demands of high-speed driving on interstate highways. At the wheels of high-speed limousines, they learn how to wind through curvy paths, break through roadblocks or barricades, and make sharp turns at high speed. To know how to escape from a possible ambush, they learn to drive in reverse at 40 miles per hour, then shift to forward drive while turning the wheel hard to either side—thus creating a perfect 180-degree turnaround (called a J-turn) so they can drive away at high speed in the opposite direction.

○ **Water safety and rescue.** Trainees at Rowley move well beyond the swimming lessons they had at FLETC. Because protectees often fly over water in helicopters, the training concentrates on teaching agents how to get out of a helicopter that has crashed in water and rolled over—the kind of accident that in 1973 cost an agent's life. In intensive simulations in a pool, they learn how to replace a breathing device underwater when its air supply is exhausted, and how to turn on a flotation apparatus that will bob them to the surface. While doing this and controlling the natural human urge to panic, they must help their protectee get safely to the surface. Practicing such water rescues, agents in the training class take turns being rescuer or victim.

○ **First aid.** Every trainee gets at least 40 hours of training as an emergency medical technician (EMT). This includes use of the various materials in a standard FAT (first-aid trauma) kit, such as oxygen bottles, splints for fractures, and medicines for burns and wounds. Correct use of a defibrillator to stabilize an irregular heartbeat is taught as part of learning cardiopulmonary resuscitation (CPR).

○ **Cover course.** Here, moving on foot along a distance of some 30 feet, trainees learn to work as teams, covering each other and taking advantage of any available cover—tree trunk, fire hydrant, refuse can, Postal Service mailbox, vending machine—to protect themselves from instructors shooting at them with paint balls.

President Barack Obama looks through binoculars in a firing range as he tours the Secret Service's James J. Rowley Training Center in Beltsville, Maryland. *(Pete Souza/The White House/Corbis)*

Much of the training occurs in a large section of the Rowley Center's 493 acres that is called the tactical village and judgmental range. The area looks like a replica of a Hollywood movie lot, with realistic buildings and streets. Here trainees, in motorcades or on foot, face tough, realistic situations as computer-controlled cutout figures (activated by instructors) suddenly accost them. Trainees must instantly make judgments as to whether the surprise means danger. For example, is the figure holding a gun or just something that looks like a gun? In one building, which can be set up to look like a hotel, trainees practice coping with indoor threats. And on a stretch of sidewalk, they learn to guard their protectee, who is moving along a rope line and shaking hands with an eager crowd. In every exercise, they build their confidence in handling the stress of sudden threats and surprise noises without hesitation to get their protectee away from the scene.

SEEING AND SNIFFING

If you take a tour of the White House, you'll notice men and women in uniform who look like members of the city's police department—but they are not. Rather, they belong to a special unit called the Secret Service Uniformed Division. It is responsible for providing security not only in and around the White House but also at the Naval Observatory (where the vice president lives), at a number of foreign missions or embassies in Washington, D.C., and at such special events as bill signings by the president, state dinners, or visits by prominent guests. Wherever admission is only through a magnetometer, members of the Uniformed Division are in charge. Their job in general is to patrol the buildings and grounds, watching for any criminal or suspicious activity or any kind of disturbance. They regularly ride bicycles on the White House pathways and motorcycles when escorting motorcades. In addition to training intensively for this work, some train for duty in special assignments such as the following:

- **Countersniper Support Unit.** These individuals have naturally superior eyesight. They train not only with a variety of weapons—including specially designed sniper rifles—but also with binoculars and night-vision scopes. Countersnipers have to be tested regularly

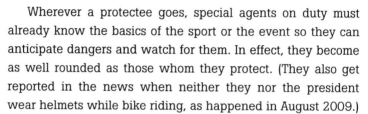

WELL ROUNDED AND WELL DRESSED

What if a president or vice president wants to go horseback riding on a California ranch? Or bike riding on Martha's Vineyard? Or is heading for the ski slopes? Or must appear at a black-tie dinner?

Wherever a protectee goes, special agents on duty must already know the basics of the sport or the event so they can anticipate dangers and watch for them. In effect, they become as well rounded as those whom they protect. (They also get reported in the news when neither they nor the president wear helmets while bike riding, as happened in August 2009.)

And when they have to go to a formal affair-of-state, where the dress code is black tie or evening gown, they must dress for the occasion. In fact, agents have to attend so many formal dinners that the agency provides, at its expense, the formal wear needed by its male and female agents.

for acrophobia (fear of heights) because they often work on rooftops. The purpose of their training is not to make them ready to fight off a major, coordinated attack. Rather, its purpose is to teach them how to pick out and hit an individual target some distance away in the midst of a crowd.

o **Canine Explosives Detection Unit.** A dog and its handler can find explosives more quickly and effectively than any human alone because a dog's sense of smell is 20 times as sensitive as a human's. The work is done best by a shorthaired breed called the Belgian Malinois (pronounced to rhyme with Illinois, with a silent s) that is built like a German shepherd and doesn't object to hot weather. Found first in Holland but now bred in the United States, the sociable dogs at the Rowley Center learn to obey verbal commands and hand signals, find missing articles, track scents on the ground, and follow the smell of an explosive to its source. They become expert at inspecting vehicles, sniffing the interior and under the uplifted

A FAMILY MEMBER, EVEN IN RETIREMENT

Bomb-sniffing dogs and their technicians become devoted pals. Trainee dog and trainee technician must successfully complete the course together, and after the first four weeks of training, a Secret Service canine says goodbye to life in a kennel and goes home every night with its technician, bonding 24 hours a day as a member of the technician's family.

Retraining comes every week for eight hours. And when the canine reaches retirement age—usually at about its 10th birthday—it spends the rest of its days living in the technician's home.

hood. When the dog finds a suspicious odor, it sits down close to the source of the smell. Canines go wherever protectees are going, checking for explosives before the protectee gets there. Because they are hearty dogs loaded with stamina and energy, they are not fazed by such big places and overwhelming crowds as they find at major events like the national political conventions held every four years.

SPECIALISTS IN FORENSIC SERVICES

Because every Secret Service agent is expected to serve in a wide variety of jobs, all are trained to understand and cope with several areas of criminal activity that do not come under the heading of protecting government leaders. These range from counterfeiting to identity theft and from insider threats to electronic crime. Another area of specialized training is threat assessment, which simply means figuring out whether an action or event is a threat to individuals or groups of people protected by the Secret Service.

If trying to find out if something is a threat, agents need to make sure that the information they are dealing with is legally permissible—that is, whether it can be used by lawyers in a case in court. If it can, it is called *forensic* evidence (a dictionary definition of *forensic* is "belonging

LEARNING HOW IN 28 INTENSIVE WEEKS

A big, strapping U.S. Naval Academy graduate who had played right guard on the football team, Scott Swantner had elected to serve in the Marine Corps. On duty as a rifle platoon commander in Iraq, he saw three fingers of his left hand blown off. Discharged, he decided to apply for admission for training as a Secret Service agent—a process that took several months and included filling out a 34-page application form, followed by passing a drug test, hearing test, vision test, and written test. He had checked in at a Secret Service field office for an initial interview, then coped with a panel of interviewers, then hosted an interview in his home. In what he called "the worst experience of my life," he had survived a polygraph test. Only one test—the physical—had left his examiners wondering. They asked Scott's Marine Corps commander about his seven-fingered officer. "He says he can physically do this," they said, "but can he? Can he still shoot?"

Disappointed by the doubts and thinking he would never be admitted to a Secret Service training class, Scott took a job at an Oakland, California, shipyard. He had worked there for two weeks when he got the call—the Secret Service, which had never before accepted a candidate with a disability like his, was ready to train him.

Over 12 weeks, Scott mastered the basic law-enforcement training at the federal school in Glynco, Georgia. Next came the 16-week course at the Rowley Training Center near Washington. In firearms class he learned to take apart, clean, and reassemble the Sig Sauer P229 pistol, the Remington 12-gauge shotgun, and the MP5 9mm submachine gun—and how to shoot for "center mass," the heart. Studying emergency medicine, he was taught not only how to treat wounds but how to deliver a baby as well. In rescue swimming, instructors drilled him in what to do or not do if a protectee falls overboard. Training on WMD (weapons of mass destruction), he learned

(continues)

(continued)

highly classified details on non-traceable toxins and other chemical, viral, and bacterial agents. Tactical driving seemed easy, despite a left hand that had only a thumb and forefinger to grip the wheel. "Run the course hard, as if you're taking the protectee to the hospital," his instructor ordered as he learned to zigzag through orange cones on 1,800 feet of blacktop and even race backward to perform a 180-degree J-turn by abruptly spinning the wheel while hitting the brakes.

On the outdoor firing range on the last day of training, Scott topped the records of all his classmates by shooting 24 of 30 shots right into the target silhouette's small heart. Who said, his classmates wondered, that an agent with only seven fingers can't shoot?[2]

to, used in, or suitable to courts of judicature or to public discussion and debate"). The Secret Service's forensic experts analyze a wide variety of evidence and testify in courtroom trials. Some of their specialties are as follows:

- **Identification.** Long known for its expertise in identifying people by their fingerprints, the Secret Service now has a wide range of services related to fingerprints. Its chemical and physical identification methods utilize state-of-the-art technology, and its specialists train not only its own field offices but other law enforcement agencies as well. They also testify as experts in local, state, and federal courts.
- **Forensic automation.** When an investigation seems to be getting nowhere, these analysts are called upon to use their computer networks to identify fingerprints and handwriting or to figure out whether identity or financial documents are counterfeit. They support all Secret Service offices and also respond to outside requests

that come in to the offices. As the duties suggest, training for this work is computer intensive.

o **Polygraph, or lie detector.** While polygraph examinations may be helpful in any case, Secret Service examiners do not usually turn to them until all other techniques of investigation have been exhausted. Using one of the world's foremost polygraph programs, the examiners are able to help the service's protective missions and criminal investigations. They also help identify desirable and undesirable candidates in the hiring process.

o **Questioned documents.** Experts trained in this field perform forensic analyses of evidence, which may include letters or other written material, found during investigations. They write reports on scientific findings, and in court cases they testify as experts. They also work in crime scene search teams and train other investigators in forensic analysis.

o **Visual information.** These graphic arts specialists know how to enhance images and pictures and analyze audio and sound. Identifying voices, modeling three-dimensional sketches of suspects or criminals, operating across the board in several media at once— such activities are all in a day's work.

On the Job

It is early autumn in 1979. The California Angels baseball team has just won the American League Western Division title. Joining the celebration in the locker room after the game is one of the team's biggest fans, former President Richard M. Nixon. With him is the director of his Secret Service security detail, Agent Michael Endicott. On the job, he has accompanied Nixon at many a baseball and football game and has often sat with him behind the dugout at New York Mets games.

Nixon is in the midst of a live radio interview with a sports broadcaster who is asking his impressions of the game. Nearby, the Angels' all-star second baseman, Bobby Grich, asks Agent Endicott if it is okay to pour beer onto Nixon's head.

"Go ahead," says Endicott, who knows Nixon well. "Knock yourself out."

Sneaking behind the former president of the United States, Grich slowly pours the beer over his head.

"He was shocked," says Endicott afterward. "He had the biggest smile on his face. He shook Grich's hand. He was part of the team's celebration."

Thanks to Agent Endicott, Nixon—who in many phases of his life has struggled against being an outsider—has become an Angels insider.[1]

"The time spent on the job protecting a president consists of a lot of long hours, long days, and longing for his family," said the wife of Special Agent Tim Greenhalgh. "But," she added, "the experiences were second to none." Her husband's experiences included 15 years in the Presidential Protective Detail (PPD), protecting Presidents George H.W. Bush, Bill Clinton, and George W. Bush, followed by several years with the first President Bush in retirement. These included salmon fishing in Alaska and exploring the sea off Kennebunkport, Maine, in the Bush cigarette boat, "The Fidelity," as well as attending the funerals of former President Ronald Reagan in Washington and Pope John Paul II in Rome. Then there were several Super Bowls and Ryder Cup golf matches and even a unique invitation for Greenhalgh's entire family to join his former boss in a private reception aboard the brand-new aircraft carrier *George H.W. Bush (CVN77)* as it was commissioned in Norfolk, Virginia, in January 2009.[2]

The fact is that if you are a Secret Service agent, the effect of being on the job continues long after you leave the job. "I can't turn off the 'what ifs' in my brain," says former agent Christopher Falkenberg. "The training is ingrained. Part of being an effective agent was having what we liked to call 'situational awareness.' It's basically nothing more than looking around your location, sizing up the people around you, and then thinking of the many things that could go wrong, and what you would do if one of those things happened."

Falkenberg says that when he travels by air he is "the guy who always pays attention to the preflight safety briefing," and that he plans what he will do if things go wrong on the flight. "I always carry a few tools," he adds. "One of my favorites is a lithium cell flashlight. When I was an agent, I found that a good flashlight is the single most useful tool on the planet. Flashlights like those aren't on the list of prohibited items."[3]

THE CONSUMMATE AGENT

Even after they have retired, very few agents talk about what it is like to be on the job. A niece of Agent James Gordon "Jeff" Jeffries said, "Jeff was the consummate Secret Service agent. He never shared much." But she knew that he had been Jacqueline Kennedy's personal bodyguard, and when her uncle was in his 80s she found a letter written to him by

Mrs. Kennedy in April 1962, when he was assigned to a different detail. "I will miss you so much," it said. "I will never meet anyone who has been as loyal and faithful as you, patient and understanding with me, so sweet and kind with my children. The President is as grateful as I am for all you did to make easy my adjustment to being guarded all the time. I will always remember you. My deepest appreciation and affection and all good wishes. Your friend, Jacqueline Kennedy."[4]

A more talkative agent was Arnold J. Lau, retired assistant director of the Secret Service, who served under Presidents Truman, Eisenhower, Kennedy, Johnson, Ford, and Carter. When Truman was living in Blair House during the major restoration of the White House, said Lau, "I'd walk a discrete distance behind him as we went from his office to his quarters. I'd also accompany him in the car when he went to play cards with his cronies."

Speaking of Eisenhower, Lau said,

> I went everywhere with him, including to the 1955 Summit Conference in Geneva, Switzerland, for his historic meeting with Prime Minister Anthony Eden of the United Kingdom, Premier Nikolai Bulganin of the Soviet Union, and Prime Minister Edgar Faure of France. We scoured every inch of Eisenhower's villa on Lake Geneva for bombs, eavesdropping devices, and anything electronic... . We were constantly researching who might have an unusual interest in the president and keeping tabs on their whereabouts. At the event itself, we were stationed at posts throughout the area, usually before dawn, and usually in frigid conditions.

President Kennedy's casual clothing and preference for not wearing a hat changed the way Secret Service agents dressed for the job. "Up until then," says Lau, "we all wore suits, white shirts, ties, and fedoras. Now we wore whatever the president wore so we would blend in."

Some major changes in Secret Service jobs came as a result of the assassinations of President Kennedy and then his brother, Robert F. Kennedy. Protection was now provided for presidential and vice-presidential candidates and their families. During President Johnson's campaign for re-election in 1964, for example, Agent Lau was frequently on duty at the president's Texas home, the LBJ Ranch. Then his job changed. He was put in charge of a comprehensive new program for training Secret Service recruits and experienced agents. On that job he developed an expanded staff of professional instructors, set up a Countersniper team trained to detect and head off would-be snipers, and created dozens of new or advanced courses.[5]

MOVING THE VICE PRESIDENT THROUGH A SPITTING MOB

H. Stuart Knight was a Secret Service agent traveling in 1958 with Vice President Richard M. Nixon and Mrs. Nixon on an eight-nation goodwill tour of South America. At their last stop, in Caracas, Venezuela, Agent Knight was on the job as the Nixons walked down the steps from their Air Force DC-6B onto a red carpet lined with Venezuelan troops. Moving toward the limousine while a band played "The Star-Spangled Banner," Knight saw a crowd of some 200 students push against the lineup of troops and begin spitting at the visitors. Then they began shouting, "Get out, Nixon!" and blowing rubber Bronx-cheer whistles as they raised bed sheets decorated with Communist slogans. Knight and other agents hurried the Nixons into separate cars as the demonstrators tried to spread banners over the windshields to blind the drivers.

The cars were halted again in heavy traffic on the Avenida Sucre. For 12 minutes an enraged, screaming mob of older men, students, and teenagers pounded Nixon's limousine with heavy clubs and threw melon-sized rocks to smash three of its windows. Shattered glass covered the vice president. One piece of glass struck the eye of Venezuelan Foreign Minister Oscar Garcia Lutin, who was sitting beside Nixon. The two Secret Service agents in the car drew their revolvers. Outside, another agent scrambled across the car's rear window to protect it. At the front bumper, other agents yanked an obstinate student from between the wheels. (Note: Typically, news reports did not reveal any agent's name. Agent Knight, however, was in the thick of it.) The mob, having thrown countless bottles and stones at the Secret Service group but failing to break down the resilience of the agents on the job, quieted. The motorcade sped to the American embassy. Next morning, the vice

(Continues on page 102)

THE JOB HAS ITS BAD DAYS, TOO

Following the assassination of President Kennedy, Agent Mike Howard was assigned an unusual job. He was put in charge of protecting the family of Lee Harvey Oswald, the accused assassin who had just been killed by Jack Ruby. For seven days, protecting the Oswalds from anyone who might seek revenge for the murder of JFK, it was Howard's job to keep them hidden in a wooded area near a prominent vacation resort.

Several years later, because Howard worked so closely with President Lyndon B. Johnson, he happened to be the agent who was with Johnson when he died.

Agents on the job got unpleasant assignments in 1972. Under orders from the Nixon administration, the Secret Service was involved in what became known as the Watergate scandal. They were required to spy on opposition presidential candidates before the Republican convention was held. After the Watergate burglary, they opened E. Howard Hunt's safe in the White House. They ran the secret audio taping system in the White House, and even tapped the telephone of Nixon's brother.

Federal rules sometimes tied the hands of agents on the job. The FBI, for example, knew that John W. Hinckley Jr. was a gun-carrying, mentally disturbed person after its agents arrested him several months before he managed to shoot President Reagan—but because a rule prohibited the sharing of information between federal agencies, no one at the FBI warned anybody at the Secret Service about Hinckley.[6]

Not every aspect of being on the job is glamorous or exciting. Agent Kristina Schmidt of the Secret Service office in Chicago, for example, was told in September 2009 that students at Genoa-Kingston High School had made threats against President Obama in an online video-game chat room. Because one of the jobs of the Secret Service is to follow up on any threat—actual or perceived—two agents were immediately dispatched to the school, where they interviewed four boys and the school superintendent.

The trip to Genoa was simply all in a day's work on the job. "I'm not going to go into the details of the investigation," said Agent Schmidt. "We determined there was no threat."

"The Secret Service let them know," said school superintendent Scott Wakeley afterward, "that making comments and threats, even in jest, about the president of the United States is not something the Secret Service takes lightly. These kids kind of thought, and I think most kids think, when they are on these online chats with open Internet connections, I think they think they are anonymous."[7]

In a similar situation a few weeks later, a posting on Facebook offered a poll on the question "Should Obama be killed?" and asked for answers no, maybe, yes, and "yes, if he cuts my health care." Over three days more than 700 responses came in, with 90 percent saying no, and even *New York Times* op-ed columnist Thomas L. Friedman wrote at length about the "really disturbing" attitude the event represented, saying, "The Secret Service is now investigating. I hope they put the jerk in jail and throw away the key."

Doing its job of investigating all threats against the president, the Secret Service found that the Facebook poll had been created by an underage teenager. Although agents interviewed the teen and his or her parents, they refused to reveal any name, age, or residence. Secret Service spokesman Ed Donovan said, "This is something we classified as a mistake on the juvenile's part."[8]

At times, the work of a Secret Service agent can be boring, but it is still necessary. For example, Michelle C. Novotny of the St. Louis Secret Service office had been an agent for five years when she was assigned duty to guard a certain flight of stairs so no one used them. She was there for 10 hours. Later, describing her job to a classroom of fourth graders, she said, "Sometimes it's lonely."[9]

(Continued from page 99)

president cut short his visit to Venezuela and, with traffic prohibited and Venezuelan army and police units guarding the 25-mile route to the airport, departed.[10]

A SHOOTING IN MARYLAND

In May 1972 Agent Nick Zarvos was a member of a Secret Service detail assigned to travel with Alabama Governor George Wallace, who was running for the Democratic nomination for president of the United States. On the job at a shopping center in Laurel, Maryland, Zarvos knew he was protecting a hard-fighting, no-holds-barred campaigner

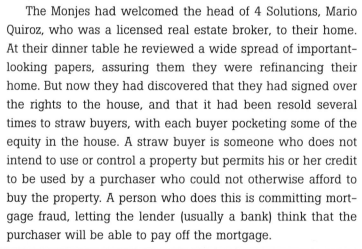

300 VICTIMIZED HOMEOWNERS

Special Agent John Joyce was in charge of the Secret Service's Tampa, Florida, field office. He was aware of a complaint by Blas and Lourdes Monje that they had been defrauded in a deal involving a mortgage on their home. They had answered an advertisement by a company called 4 Solutions. The ad appealed to Hispanic couples like the Monjes who wanted to refinance their houses to avoid foreclosure.

The Monjes had welcomed the head of 4 Solutions, Mario Quiroz, who was a licensed real estate broker, to their home. At their dinner table he reviewed a wide spread of important-looking papers, assuring them they were refinancing their home. But now they had discovered that they had signed over the rights to the house, and that it had been resold several times to straw buyers, with each buyer pocketing some of the equity in the house. A straw buyer is someone who does not intend to use or control a property but permits his or her credit to be used by a purchaser who could not otherwise afford to buy the property. A person who does this is committing mortgage fraud, letting the lender (usually a bank) think that the purchaser will be able to pay off the mortgage.

whose "segregation forever" attitude produced extremely passionate opponents and supporters. And he knew that Wallace knew he was always in danger, for the 600-pound lectern he took with him to stand behind wherever he spoke was bulletproof, and so was the unwieldy vest he wore in his public appearances.

The day, May 5, was extremely humid; the heat so overwhelming that Wallace decided not to wear his heavy bulletproof vest. Zarvos and the other agents watched nearby on the shopping plaza's temporary stage as the governor, his shirt soaked in perspiration, ended a fiery 50-minute speech amid deafening applause. As Wallace then headed down steps toward a crowd of some 2,000, Zarvos and other agents

While the Monjes went to court to get a judgment against 4 Solutions, Special Agent Joyce directed an investigation of the mortgage fraud. Agents found that at least 300 homeowners had been victimized by Mario Quiroz and his partner, Jose Oliveri. The homeowners, most of whom needed money, had thought they were refinancing but were duped into signing over the rights to their homes so 4 Solutions could sell them without telling the owners. Some straw buyers, Special Agent Joyce noticed, had each bought several homes, and at least one had obtained eight. Twelve banks or other financial institutions had lost some $8 million. And Quiroz and Oliveri were nowhere to be found.

It took two years to catch up with them. "These guys were on our international most-wanted list," said Joyce, "and some of our agents in Peru were contacted with information as to their whereabouts." As a result of that informant's tip, both men were arrested in Peru in October 2009. Held there, they waited while Special Agent Joyce, on the job in the Tampa office, alerted U.S. officials to get them back to the U.S. on charges of mail fraud, wire fraud, money laundering, and conspiracy.[11]

surrounded him, ready to escort him to his car. But so many supporters were calling to Wallace and reaching out to shake his hand that he
turned, removing his suit jacket and rolling up his sleeves, to greet those
pushing against a rope barrier. Instantly he was in his favorite part of
campaigning: grinning a "howdy" and a "how're ya doin'?" to countless
handshakers.

In less than a minute, Zarvos saw it all end. A blond man in the
crowd's second row—a foot and a half from Wallace—reached forward
with a pistol and fired. The governor fell backward. Five more shots
were fired. Agent Nick Zarvos dropped to the ground, shot in the
throat.

Governor Wallace survived, thanks to emergency room doctors who
saved his life on the operating table, but he was permanently paralyzed
from the waist down. The blond man, Arthur Bremer, was found guilty
of attempted assassination and sentenced to 63 years in prison. Nick
Zarvos survived, joining the list of the very few Secret Service agents
who have been wounded on the job.[12]

The Wallace experience convinced the Secret Service that crowds
rallying to hear presidential candidates, or gathering for any similar
event, must pass through magnetometers, which would have detected
Bremer's gun.

GUNFIRE AND BLOODSHED AT BLAIR HOUSE

At about 2:00 P.M. on November 1, 1950, Special Agent Floyd Boring
was on the job, along with Secret Service White House Police Private
Joseph Davidson, in the east security booth in front of Blair House on
Pennsylvania Avenue. President and Mrs. Truman were living there
while, across the street, the White House was being renovated. The
president was napping upstairs. Boring was talking with Washington
Police Officer Donald Birdzell a few feet away on Blair House's first step.
Suddenly he saw one of the area's passersby stop eight feet from Birdzell.
In a single motion the man pulled out an automatic pistol. It clicked,
then fired. The bullet hit Birdzell in his right knee. Instantly, Boring and
Davidson pulled out their own guns and fired at the stranger.

Copr. 1950 by News Syndicate Co. Inc. NEW YORK'S PICTURE NEWSPAPER Trade Mark Reg. U. S. Pat. Off.

Vol. 32. No. 112 New York 17, Thursday, November 2, 1950★ 96 Main+20 Brooklyn+4 Kings Pages 3 Cents IN CITY | 4 CENTS | 5 CENTS LIMITS | in Suburbs | Elsewhere

2 DIE, 3 SHOT AS PAIR TRY TO KILL TRUMAN

—Story on Page 3

Death at Truman's Doorstep. Griselio Torresola [▲], one of two men who tried to shoot their way into Blair House in assassination attempt on President Truman, lies dead under hedge outside temporary White House. His gun (arrow) lies in grass. His companion, Oscar Collazo, was wounded. Three White House guards were also wounded (one of them fatally). Despite attempt on his life, Truman went on to memorial service for Sir John Dill at Arlington Cemetery [→]. —*Story on page 3*

(More pictures of attempted assassination in centerfold)

A *Daily News* (New York) front page dated November 2, 1950, breaks the news of the attempt on President Harry Truman's life at Blair House in Washington, D.C. Secret Service White House Police Private Leslie Coffelt lost his life protecting the president. *(NY Daily News via Getty Images)*

At the same moment, Special Agent Boring realized another stranger was at the west security booth, shooting bullet after bullet into Secret Service White House Police Private Leslie Coffelt's abdomen. Boring saw the officer collapse onto the floor of the sentry box. Now, as this second stranger turned and shot at White House Police Officer Joseph Downs, Boring saw the wounded Birdzell crawl into the street to draw the first stranger's attention away from Blair House. At the same time, the severely wounded Private Coffelt struggled to his feet, leaning against the sentry box, and fired carefully into the second stranger's head, killing him instantly. Simultaneously, Boring and the other agents and officers kept firing at the first stranger until he fell to the ground. Altogether, perhaps 30 seconds had passed. Twenty-seven shots had been exchanged. Upstairs, Agent Stewart Stout, hearing the shots, had stood at the president's door, Thompson submachine gun in hand. Private Coffelt died in surgery three hours later.

An official investigation revealed that the attacking strangers were Oscar Collazo and Griselo Torresola, a pair of Puerto Ricans who intended to kill President Truman in order to increase American awareness of their island's demand for independence. They had thought it would be easy to down a couple of guards at the Blair House door.

Refusing to let his lawyers plead insanity, Collazo was sentenced to death, but, with his sentence commuted by President Truman, lived in prison until 1979. He was then returned to Puerto Rico, where he died in 1994.

The Future of the Secret Service

In October 2009 the *Boston Globe* reported that "The unprecedented number of death threats against President Obama, a rise in racist hate groups, and a new wave of antigovernment fervor threaten to overwhelm the U.S. Secret Service, according to government officials and reports, raising new questions about the 144-year-old agency's overall mission."

The newspaper quoted from an internal report issued by the Congressional Research Service that said, "If there were an evaluation of the service's two missions, it might be determined that it is ineffective... to conduct its protection mission and investigate financial crimes." A Secret Service spokesman replied immediately, saying, "In the longest and most expensive campaign in history, the Secret Service has proven it can maintain its dual mission of both protecting individuals and conducting criminal investigations. The Secret Service had forfeitures totaling $140 million and investigated the largest data breach in history. There were also zero arrests at the largest inauguration ever."[1]

Looking at the *Boston Globe*'s comments, it is hard to find "new questions about the 144-year-old agency's overall mission." Choosing at random a typical day—June 9, 2010—more than six months after the newspaper published its criticism, the following events and activities can be found:

- In Louisville, Kentucky, a federal grand jury indicted eight suspects accused by the Secret Service of stealing the identities of about 200 people. "The different twist," said Agent Paul Johnson, "is that this group was very organized in the sense of using identity theft as a means to get prescription drugs."[2]
- In Kalamazoo, Michigan, President Barack Obama shook the hand of each Central High School graduate, all of whom had earlier been asked for birthdates, Social Security numbers, and citizenship status so the Secret Service could perform background checks before the president spoke at their commencement ceremony. Entering audience members were screened by Secret Service magnetometers.
- At the request of the Secret Service, Pinehurst, North Carolina, police arrested a local resident at his home, charged him with using a computer to communicate threats to the president of the United States, and held him in jail pending interrogation by Secret Service agents. Pinehurst Police Department Captain Floyd Thomas said the same man "was arrested, if I am remembering correctly, by Secret Service about a year ago for the same thing."[3]
- Police in the cities of Marshall and Battle Creek, Michigan, along with state police, joined the Secret Service in warning businesses not to accept $50 bills because they could be counterfeit. The police, checking on bills presented at local gas stations, suspected that a group of local people were bleaching five-dollar bills and converting them to $50 bills. "They kind of looked funny," said Battle Creek Detective Sergeant Austin Simmons.[4]
- Former U.S. Secret Service Agent Larry Stewart testified as a forensics expert in a courtroom in Munich, Germany. There former Ohio autoworker John Demjanjuk, a native of Ukraine who was charged with 28,000 counts of accessory to murder, was being tried on allegations that during World War II he was a guard at the Nazis' Sorbibor death camp. In 2000 Agent Stewart had examined Demjanjuk's Nazi-issued identity card, which indicated that the defendant was a guard at the camp, and found it genuine.
- In Harveys Lake, Pennsylvania, near Wilkes-Barre, the Secret Service charged a trained paralegal with theft of $2 million over four years. The suspect, who was the owner of a title insurance company and vice-chairman of the local Republican party, was accused of

A Secret Service special agent holds a plastic bag with rejected counterfeit $100 and $20 United States Federal Reserve notes alongside evidence displayed during a news conference at the Secret Service offices in Los Angeles in May 2008. Five people, including the man who admitted to being the printer, were arrested in relation to a counterfeit currency operation that used inkjet and laser printers to produce millions of dollars in fake bills. *(AP Photo/Damian Dovarganes)*

neglecting to file critical property-transaction documents, not paying off sellers' mortgages with funds in hand, stealing money from escrow accounts, failure to use premiums to purchase title insurance policies, lying about disbursement of funds, and forging documents to gain access to her daughter's checking account.

- In Washington, D.C., handyman Gary Gionet headed home to Dallas, Texas, after extensive questioning by Secret Service agents. Over the previous weekend, he had covered his yellow, box truck

A group of Secret Service agents brace themselves against the propeller wash from Marine One, the presidential helicopter. *(Jim Young/Reuters/Corbis)*

with messages to President Obama offering to advise the president on how to stanch the flow of oil in the Gulf of Mexico from the explosion of the BP Deepwater Horizon drill. He then drove the truck around Washington, but when he reached Constitution Avenue near the White House he was stopped by police and Secret Service agents. "They asked, 'What would I do if I didn't get to speak to the president?'" said Gionet later. "I said I'd be disappointed and I'd go home." After a long interview, the Secret Service released Gionet but told him to leave the White House area because of restrictions on large trucks and on stopping or parking nearby.[5]

In fulfilling its overall mission during a given 24-hour period, these were among the duties that were all in a day's work for the Secret Service. It appears that the Secret Service is fulfilling its responsibilities as usual, despite the record-breaking number of threats it must investigate.

Chronology

1865	Secret Service is founded on July 5 in Washington, D.C., to curb counterfeit money; Chief William P. Wood sworn in
1867	Responsibilities broaden to include "detecting persons perpetrating frauds against the government," such as law-breaking distillers, mail robbers, smugglers, and land frauds
1877	Congress passes an act prohibiting counterfeiting of any coin
1883	Secret Service officially becomes a distinct organization within the Treasury Department
1894	President Grover Cleveland informally protected part time by Secret Service
1895	Congress prohibits counterfeiting or possession of counterfeit stamps
1901	After assassination of President William McKinley, Congress informally requests Secret Service protection for U.S. presidents
1902	Two operatives assigned to White House detail as Secret Service assumes full-time responsibility for protecting the president
1906	Congress provides funds for presidential protection. Secret Service begins investigating western land frauds
1907	First operative killed in line of duty, Joseph A. Walker, murdered November 3 while working on land fraud case
1908	Secret Service begins protecting the president-elect; President Theodore Roosevelt forms the Federal

	Bureau of Investigation (FBI) by transferring eight agents from the Secret Service
1913	Congress authorizes permanent protection for the president and president-elect
1915	President Woodrow Wilson directs the secretary of the treasury to order Secret Service investigation of espionage in the United States
1917	Congress authorizes permanent protection for the president's immediate family and makes threats against the president a federal violation
1922	President Warren G. Harding requests the creation of White House Police Force
1930	Secret Service begins to supervise White House Police
1950	Protecting President Harry S. Truman at Blair House on November 1, White House Police officer Leslie Coffelt is killed by Puerto Rican nationalists
1951	Congress permanently authorizes Secret Service protection of the president and family, president-elect, and vice president if he requests it
1961	Congress authorizes protection of former presidents
1962	Congress expands coverage to include the vice president or next officer to succeed the president, and the vice-president-elect
1963	Congress passes legislation to protect Mrs. John F. Kennedy and her minor children for two years
1965	Congress authorizes protection of former presidents and their spouses during their lifetimes, and minor children until age 16
1968	Following the assassination of Robert F. Kennedy, Congress authorizes protection of major presidential and vice-presidential candidates and nominees, as well as protection of widows of presidents until their deaths or remarriages, and their children until age 16
1970	White House Police Force is renamed the Executive Protective Service; its responsibilities increase to include protection of diplomatic missions in the Washington, D.C., area

1971	Congress authorizes Secret Service protection for visiting heads of foreign states or governments, or other official guests
1975	Executive Protective Service duties are expanded to include protection of foreign diplomatic missions throughout the United States and its territories
1977	On November 15 the Executive Protective Service is renamed the Secret Service Uniformed Division
1984	Congress makes the fraudulent use of credit and debit cards a federal violation, and authorizes the Secret Service to investigate credit and debit card fraud, federal-interest computer fraud, and fraudulent identification documents
1986	A presidential directive authorizes Secret Service protection for the accompanying spouse of the head of a foreign state or government
1997	Congress passes legislation providing that presidents elected after January 1, 1997, receive Secret Service protection for 10 years after leaving office; those elected before January 1, 1997, receive lifetime protection
2000	Congress passes the Presidential Threat Protection Act, authorizing the Secret Service to participate in the planning, coordination, and implementation of security operations at special events of national significance, as determined by the president
2002	The Department of Homeland Security is established; on March 1 the U.S. Secret Service is transferred there from the Department of the Treasury
2004	Veteran Agent Barbara Riggs is the first woman in Secret Service history to be named deputy director
2006	To fight high-tech, computer-based crimes, the network of Electronic Crimes Task Forces expands from 15 to 24 nationwide
2007	In the earliest start of Secret Service protection for any presidential candidate in history, protection begins in May for Illinois Senator Barack Obama

Endnotes

Chapter 1

1. "Frequently Asked Questions," Secret Service Official Web Site, http://www.secretservice.gov/faq.shtml#faq8 (Accessed July 6, 2010).

Chapter 2

1. Earle Looker, *The White House Gang* (New York: Fleming H. Revell Company, 1929), 193.

Chapter 3

1. Holly Bailey, "Where Everybody Knows Your Name," *Newsweek*, May 4, 2009, http://www.newsweek.com/id/195086 (Posted April 26, 2009).
2. Henry M. Holden, *To Be A U.S. Secret Service Agent* (St. Paul, Minn.: Zenith Press, 2006); Anonymous, "Names Used by the Secret Service," Presidential Codenames, http://presidentialcodenames.com (Accessed May 11, 2009).
3. Christopher Reich, "They'd Take a Bullet For The President," *Parade*, January 4, 2009, http://www.parade.com/news/2009/01/they-would-give-their-lives-for-the-president.html (Accessed January 1, 2009).
4. Rebecca Cole, "Congress members arrested in Darfur protest," *Los Angeles Times*, April 28, 2009, http://www.latimes.com/news/nationworld/nation/la-na-darfur-protest28-2009apr28,0,5399372.story (Posted April 28, 2009).
5. Maureen Sieh, "Security Measures Tight for Vice President Biden's Talk at Syracuse University Commencement," *Syracuse Post-Standard*, May 7, 2009, http://www.syracuse.com/news/index.ssf/2009/05/security_measures_tight_for_vi.html (Posted May 7, 2009); Marnie Eisenstadt, "University Hospital ready for vice president in Syracuse," *Syracuse Post-Standard*, May 10, 2009, http://www.syracuse.com:80/news/index.ssf/2009/05/university_hospital_ready_for.html (Posted May 11, 2009).
6. Christopher Reich, "They'd Take a Bullet For The President," *Parade*, January 4, 2009, http://www.parade.com/news/2009/01/they-would-give-their-lives-for-the-president.html (Accessed January 1, 2009).
7. Oliver Mathenge, "G20 summit: Lengths they go to secure Obama," *Daily Nation*, April 2, 2009, http://www.nation.co.ke/News/-/1056/555884/-/u3qmg4/-/index.html (Posted April 1, 2009).
8. United Rail Passenger Alliance, Inc., Jacksonville, Florida, February 6, 2009, http://transitinutah.

blogspot.com/2009/02/this-week-in-amtrak.html (Accessed February 8, 2009).

9. About the White House, "Air Force One," http://www.whitehouse.gov/about/air-force-one (Accessed May 20, 2009).

10. Henry M. Holden, *To Be A U.S. Secret Service Agent* (St. Paul, Minn.: Zenith Press, 2006).

11. Stephen Losey, "FDR, Al Capone's armored car, and oddball procurement rules of the '40s," FederalTimes.com, July 14, 2009, http://blogs.federaltimes.com/federal-times-blog/2009/07/14/fdr-al-capones-armored-car-and-oddball-procurement-rules-of-the-40s (Posted July 14, 2009).

12. Philip H. Melanson, and Peter F. Stevens, *The Secret Service: The Hidden History of an Enigmatic Agency* (New York: MJF Books, 2002).

Chapter 4

1. Jamie Nash, "Secret Service moves forward with investigation begun in Splendora," *Montgomery County News*, March 18, 2009.

2. *United States Secret Service: Fiscal Year 2008 Annual Report* (Washington, D.C.: U.S. Department of Homeland Security, 2008).

3. Fedpoint, "How Currency Gets into Circulation," Federal Reserve Bank of New York, http://www.newyorkfed.org/aboutthefed/fedpoint/fed01.html (Accessed June 15, 2009).

4. *United States Secret Service: Fiscal Year 2008 Annual Report* (Washington, D.C.: U.S. Department of Homeland Security, 2008); Josh Meyer, "U.S. officials troubled by

fake currency flowing from Peru," *Los Angeles Times*, September 13, 2009, http://articles.latimes.com/2009/sep/13/nation/na-counterfeit13 (Accessed September 13, 2009).

5. Teresa Stepzinski, "Brunswick church hurting from sin of greed," *The Florida Times-Union*, March 17, 2009; "Former Brunswick day care director sentenced to federal prison," *The Florida Times-Union*, June 9, 2009.

6. The Associated Press, "Woman charged with turning $801 check into $6,801," *ABC News*, December 17, 2008, http://abcnews.go.com/WaterCooler/wireStory?id=6474740 (Posted December 17, 2008).

7. Patricia M. Gonzalez, "Biscayne Park police charge group with stealing from village bank account," *Miami Herald*, March 20, 2009.

8. Timothy O'Connor, "Chappaqua CPA charged with stealing clients' tax refunds," *The Journal News*, February 3, 2009, http://search.lohud.com/sp?skin=100&aff=1117&keywords=Chappaqua%20CPA%20charged%20with%20stealing%20clients'%20tax%20refunds (Posted February 3, 2009); "Chappaqua CPA admits stealing $300G in tax refunds," *The Journal News*, April 21, 2009, http://m.lohud.com/news.jsp?key=234748&p=1 (Posted April 21, 2009).

9. Michele Masterson, "Anti-Scientology Hacker Admits Attacks," *The Channel Wire*, May 12, 2009, http://www.crn.com/security/217400448 (Posted May 12, 2009).

10. Jennifer Clark, "U.S. and Europe Jointly Establish Cyber-Crime Force," *The Wall Street Journal*, June 30, 2009.

11. Lolita C. Baldor, "Federal agency Web sites knocked out by massive, resilient cyber attack," *The Los Angeles Times*, July 7, 2009, http://www.latimes.com/news/nation-wide/politics/wire/sns-ap-cyber-attack,1,3110503.story (Posted July 8, 2009); "Governments hit by cyber attack," *BBC News*, July 8, 2009, http://news.bbc.co.uk/go/pr/fr/-/2/hi/technology/8139821.stm (Posted July 8, 2009); Choe Sang-Hun and John Markoff, "Cyberattacks Jam Government and Commercial Web Sites in U.S. and South Korea," *The New York Times*, July 9, 2009, http://www.nytimes.com/2009/07/09/technology/09cyber.html?_r=1 (Posted July 9, 2009).

12. Anonymous Contributor, "4 Charged in Syracuse CC Fraud," *The Gouveneur Times*, May 11, 2009, http://www.gouverneurtimes.com/index.php?option=com_content&view=article&id=3435:4-romanians-charged-in-syracuse-cc-fraud-&catid=62:new-york-state-news&Itemid=175 (Posted May 11, 2009).

13. Don Thompson, "Calif. Man charged with dealing, selling IDs," *The San Jose Mercury News*, March 27, 2009, http://mercurynews.com/news/ci_12012334?nclick_check=1 (Posted March 27, 2009).

14. Freeman Klopoff, "Secret Service: Restaurant waiters key players in credit card scam," *WTOP News*, March 30, 2009, http://www.wtop.com/?nid=25&sid=1636329, (Posted March 30, 2009).

15. Kim Zetter, "Secret Service Operative Moonlights as Identify Thief," *Wired News*, June 6, 2007, http://www.wired.com/print/politics/law/news/2007/06/secret_service (Accessed October 6, 2008).

16. Reuters, "Nine Charged in Multi-Million Dollar Leased-Funds Accounts Fraud Conspiracy," *PRNewswire-USNewswire*, March 31, 2009, http://www.reuters.com/article/pressRelease/idUS256489+31-Mar-2009+PRN20090331 (Accessed April 1, 2009).

17. Torsten Ove, "Hacker pleads guilty to stealing 1.8 million credit card numbers," *Pittsburgh Post-Gazette*, June 30, 2009, http://www.post-gazette.com/pg/09181/980704-84.stm (Posted June 30, 2009).

Chapter 5

1. Bill Dedman, "Secret Service Is Seeking Pattern for School Killers," *The New York Times*, June 21, 1999, http://www.nytimes.com/1999/06/21/us/secret-service-is-seeking-pattern-for-school-killers.html (Accessed July 17, 2009).

2. Bill Dedman, "Deadly Lessons – School Shooters: Secret Service Findings," Know Gangs, October 15, 2000, http://www.knowgangs.com/school_resources/deadlylessons.pdf (Accessed June 8, 2009).

3. Bill Dedman, "Secret Service Is Seeking Pattern for School Killers," *The New York Times*, June 21, 1999.

4. Byron "Putt" Riddle, "Data Forensics New Field for Wells

Brothers," *The Mexia Daily News*, http://www.mexiadailynews.com/?Story=985 (Posted March 13, 2009).

5. Press release, "Secret Service and CERT® Coordination Center Release Comprehensive Report Analyzing Insider Threats to Banking and Finance Sector," Washington, D.C., August 2004; Press release, "Secret Service and CERT Release Report Analyzing Acts of Insider Sabotage Via Computer Systems in Critical Infrastructure Sectors," Washington, D.C., May 16, 2008; Executive summary, "Insider Threat Study: Illicit Cyber Activity in the Information Technology and Telecommunications Sector," Washington, D.C., January 2008; Executive Summary, "Insider Threat Study: Illicit Cyber Activity in the Government Sector," Washington, D.C., January 2008

Chapter 6

1. Bonnie Pfister, "Unknowns Abound; So Do Opportunities," *Pittsburgh G-20 Partnership*, August 17, 2009, https://www.pittsburghg20.org/Articles/081709.aspx (Accessed August 19, 2009); Jerome L. Sherman, "G-20: Police seek One Voice; protesters plan many," *Pittsburgh Post-Gazette*, July 16, 2009, http://www.post-gazette.com/pg/09197/984332-53.stm (Accessed July 16, 2009); Barb Hickey, "Marches planned for G-20 summit," *Pittsburgh City Buzz Examiner*, August 16, 2009, http://www.examiner.com/x-17696-Pittsburgh-City-Buzz-Examiner~y2009m8d16-

Marches-planned-for-G20-summit (Accessed August 17, 2009).

2. Brian Westley, "Officials apologize for inauguration shut out," The Associated Press, ABC News, March 26, 2009, http://abcnews.go.com/Politics/WireStory?id=7172038&page=2 (Posted March 26, 2009); Nikki Schwab, "Secret Service Concedes Inauguration Crowd Slip-Ups," *U.S. News & World Report*, March 26, 2009, http://www.usnews.com/blogs/washington-whispers/2009/03/26/secret-service-concedes-inauguration-crowd-slip-ups.html (Posted March 26, 2009).

3. Jose Fermoso, "President Obama Wears Bullet-Resistant Suit at Inaugural," Wired.com, January 21, 2009, http://www.wired.com/gadgetlab/2009/01/president-oba-1 (Accessed January 24, 2009).

4. Julian E. Barnes, "General: Inauguration Day will see military on high alert in D.C.," *Chicago Tribune*, December 18, 2008, http://articles.chicagotribune.com/2008-12-18/news/0812170856_1_inauguration-of-barack-obama-inaugural-events-inauguration-day (Posted December 18, 2009); Jeanne Meserve, "Officials shoring up inaugural traffic security plans," CNNPolitics.com, January 13, 2009, http://www.cnn.com/2009/POLITICS/01/13/inauguration.security (Accessed January 15, 2009); Greg Gordon, "Obama to become president amid tightest security ever," *Lexington Herald Leader*, January 8, 2009, http://www.mcclatchydc.

com/2009/01/08/59302/obama-to-become-president-amid.html (Accessed January 12, 2009); Eileen Sullivan, "Inauguration security center to go live Saturday," Associated Press, January 17, 2009, http://www.google.com/hostednews/ap/article/AleqM5i-pedFEvhCtlizQ2Fxys51DiaT1LA (Posted January 17, 2009); Joel Achenbach, "Alphabet Soup of Agencies in Charge," *The Washington Post*, January 17, 2009, http://www.washingtonpost.com/wp-dyn/content/article/2009/01/16/AR2009011604465.html (Posted January 17, 2009); Peulta Dvorak, "'Label Your Kids' Among Tips Suggested by Swearing-in Vets," *The Washington Post*, January 18, 2009, http://www.washington-post.com/wp-dyn/content/article/2009/01/17/AR2009011702401.html (Posted January 18, 2009).

5. Sam Jones, Jenny Percival, and Paul Lewis, "G20 protests: riot police clash with demonstrators," *Guardian News and Media Limited*, April 1, 2009, http://www.guardian.co.uk/world/2009/apr/01/g20-summit-protests (Accessed August 20, 2009); "U.S. Secret Service Will Head Up Pittsburgh G-20 Security," *ThePittsburghChannel.com*, June 25, 2009, http://www.thepittsburghchannel.com/print/19860892/detail.html (Posted June 25, 2009); The Associated Press, "G-20 meeting in PA. May require 4,000 officers," *philly.com*, June 28, 2009, http://www.philly.com/philly/wires/ap/news/state/pennsylvania/20090628apg20meetinginpamayrequire4000officers.html (Posted June 28, 2009); Tim Puko, "Biden's recent

visit causes downtown gridlock," *Pittsburgh Tribune-Review*, July 3, 2009, http://www.pittsburghlive.com/x/pittsburghtrib/obituaries/news/s_632270.html (Accessed July 4, 2009); Associated Press, "Pittsburgh schools to close for G-20 summit," *philly.com*, August 20, 2009, http://www.philly.com/philly/wires/ap/news/state/pennsylvania/20090820_ap_pittsburghschoolstocloseforg20summit.html (Posted August 22, 2009); Dan Nephin, "Pittsburgh approves permit for G-20 rally," *philly.com*, August 21, 2009, http://www.philly.com/philly/wires/ap/news/state/pennsylvania/20090821_ap_pittsburghapprovespermitforg20rally.html (Posted August 21, 2009).

Chapter 7

1. Laura Blumenfeld, "Threat Theater: For the actors, it's a living. For the officers, it's a test of nerve," *The Washington Post*, August 17, 2009, http://www.washingtonpost.com/wp-dyn/content/article/2009/08/16/AR2009081602250.html (Accessed August 17, 2009).

2. Laura Blumenfeld, "The Making of an Agent," *The Washington Post*, July 26, 2009, http://www.washingtonpost.com/wp-dyn/content/article/2009/07/17/AR2009071701785.html (Accessed July 24, 2009).

Chapter 8

1. Gail Wood, "St. Martin's grad to talk on his life in Secret Service," *The News Tribune*, August 26, 2009.

2. Kathleen L. Radcliff, "Dublin man enjoyed his Secret Service assign-

ment," *Columbus Local News*, February 10, 2009.

3. Christopher Falkenberg, as told to Joan Raymond, "FREQUENT FLIER: Always Mindful of Finding the Nearest Exit," *The New York Times,* September 8, 2009, http://www.nytimes. com/2009/09/08/business/08flier. html?_r=l (Accessed September 8. 2009).

4. Ruth Baum Bigus, "Tribute: James Gordon Jeffries protected presidents as Secret Service agent," *Kansas City Star*, January 31, 2009.

5. Rita Borden, "Obama triggers memories for former agent," *The Chapel Hill News*, February 25, 2009, http://www.chapelhillnews. com/news/v-print/story/42876. html (Accessed February 26, 2009).

6. Patricia Sullivan, "Agent Was Secret Service's 15th Director," *The Washington Post,* September 12, 2009.

7. Kate Schott, "Students' threats against Obama not credible," *Northwest Herald,* October 1, 2009.

8. David Jackson, "Secret Service IDs kid for Facebook 'assassination poll' – no changes," *USA Today*, October 1, 2009; Thomas L. Friedman, "Where Did 'We' Go?" *The New York Times*, September 30, 2009; Marc Lizoain, "Should Obama Be Assassinated? Tom Friedman is Shocked!" *The Faster Times*, October 1, 2009, http://thefastertimes. com/publicopinion/2009/10/01/ should-obama-be-assassinated- tom-friedman-is-shocked (Accessed October 2, 2009).

9. Maria Baran, "Secret Service agent details how it's done," *Belleville News-Democrat*, February 4, 2009.

10. Patricia Sullivan, "Agent Was Secret Service's 15th Director," *The Washington Post*, September 12, 2009, http://www.washington-post.com/wp-dyn/content/article/2009/09/11/AR2005 (Accessed September 12, 2009); Tad Szulc, "U.S. Flies Troops to Caribbean as Mobs Attack Nixon in Caracas; Eisenhower Demands His Safety," *The New York Times*, May 14, 1958; Tac Szulc, "Nixon in San Juan," *The New York Times*, May 15, 1958; Yisrael Midad, "President Bush is Coming: Remember Nixon?" *My Right Word*, December 27, 2007, http://myrightword. blogspot.com/2007/12/president-bush-is-coming-remember-nixon. html (Accessed September 16, 2009).

11. Shannon Behnken, "2 Held in Peru Accused of Fraud," *TampaBayOnline – Tampa Tribune*, October 8, 2009; Jessica Vander Velde, "Fugitives found, arrested in Peru," *St. Petersburg Times*, October 7, 2009, http://www. tampabay.com/news/publicsafety/ crime/tampa-mortgage-fraud-suspects-arrested-in-peru/1042377 (Accessed October 8, 2009).

12. Philip H. Melanson, Ph.D., with Peter R. Stevens, *The Secret Service* (New York: MJF Books, 2002), 92–99.

Chapter 9

1. Bryan Bender, "Secret Service strained as leaders face more threats," *The Boston Globe*, October 18, 2009, http://www.boston. com/news/nation/washington/

articles/2009/10/18/secret_service_under_strain_as_leaders_face_more_threats?mode=PF (Accessed October 18, 2009); Fox News, "Secret Service Refutes Report Claiming Agency Stretched Too Thin," FoxNews.com, October 18, 2009, http://www.foxnews.com/politics/2009/10/18/secret-service-refutes-report-claiming-agency-stretched (Accessed October 19, 2009).

2. "Secret Service: Ring First Of Its Kind In Louisville Area," WLKY, Louisville, Kentucky, June 9, 2010, http://www.wlky.com/news/23851825/detail.html (Accessed July 6, 2010).

3. "Pinehurst Man Charged With Threatening President," *The Pilot*," Pinehurst, NC, June 9, 2010, http://www.thepilot.com/news/2010/jun/09/pinehurst-man-charged-with-threatening-president/ (Accessed July 6, 2010).

4. Henry Erb, "Police work to control counterfeit $50s," WOOD-TV, Calhoun County, Michigan, June 9, 2010, http://www.woodtv.com/dpp/news/local/kalamazoo_and_battle_creek/Police-Counterfeit-bills-pass-pen-test (Accessed July 6, 2010).

5. Corey Friedman, "Gaston man says he can stop BP oil spill, seeks sitdown with Obama," *Gaston Gazette*, Gaston, Texas, June 9, 2010.

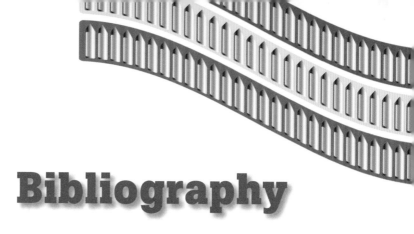

Bibliography

Holden, Henry M. *To Be a U.S. Secret Service Agent.* St. Paul, Minn.: Zenith, 2006.

Melanson, Philip H., Ph.D., with Peter F. Stevens. *The Secret Service: The Hidden History of an Enigmatic Agency.* New York: MJF Books, 2002.

Petro, Joseph, with Jeffrey Robinson. *Standing Next to History: An Agent's Life Inside the Secret Service.* New York: Thomas Dunne Books, St. Martin's Press, 2005.

United States Secret Service Fiscal Year 2008 Annual Report. Washington, D.C.: U.S. Department of Homeland Security, 2008.

Further Resources

Print

Bolden, Abraham. *The Echo from Dealey Plaza: The true story of the first African American on the White House Secret Service detail and his quest for justice after the assassination of JFK*. New York: Harmony, 2008. Reviewing this book, *Publishers Weekly*, the journal of the publishing business, said, "Conspiracy theories haunt the Kennedy assassination; Bolden offers a new one, concerning discrimination and evidence suppression…a world of duplicitous charges and disappearing documents fit for a movie thriller."

Braver, Adam. *November 22, 1963*. Portland, Ore.: Tin House Books, 2008. Reading this book takes you almost minute-by-minute through the day of the Kennedy assassination. While the story blends fact and some fiction, it is loaded with specific details and compelling emotion.

Endicott, Michael. *Walking with Presidents—Stories from Inside the Perimeter*. Charleston, S.C.: Booksurge, 2009. This book is by a retired agent who was known for quick and accurate decisions, a keen eye for detail, and top-notch planning skills. It reveals what it was like to protect Secretary of State Henry Kissinger and President Richard M. Nixon in the intense days of the Watergate scandal and Nixon's resignation, plus an up-close look at California Governor Ronald Reagan as he ran for the presidency.

Kersten, Jason. *The Art of Making Money: The Story of a Master Counterfeiter*. New York: Gotham Books, 2009. This true story of skilled artisan Art Williams tells how he used modern copying and printing technology to crèate extremely accurate fake money that included colored fibers and false watermarks—and how, after passing off or selling millions of good-looking but phony dollars, he wound up in jail.

Kessler, Ronald. *In the President's Secret Service: Behind the Scenes with Agents in the Line of Fire and the Presidents They Protect*. New York: Crown, 2009. The newsman who authored this book claims he interviewed more than 100 past and present agents before filling its pages with their gossip and complaints. However, he lists no sources for his information and includes no endnotes to authenticate what the *Washington Post* calls "the book's inane and endless anecdotes."

Online

Secret Service Recruitment Program
http://www.secretservice.gov/opportunities_interns.shtml
Visit this site for information about careers in the Secret Service.

United States Secret Service
http://www.secretservice.gov
This is a comprehensive Web site that includes many pages of useful information and links to further sources.

Index

About the Author

Bernard Ryan Jr. has authored, coauthored, or ghostwritten 36 books on such topics as biography, early childhood education, community service for teens, career guides in the fields of advertising and journalism, courtroom trials, and personal financial planning, including *The Poisoned Life of Mrs. Maybrick*, about an American woman who, in Liverpool, England, in 1889, was the defendant in one of history's great murder trials. Mr. Ryan has written many articles for magazines and newspapers. He is a graduate of Princeton University. A native of Albion, New York, he lives with his wife, Jean Bramwell Ryan, in Southbury, Connecticut. They have two daughters and two grandchildren.